Quantum Success

8 KEY CATALYSTS
TO SHIFT YOUR ENERGY
INTO DYNAMIC FOCUS

Quantum
Success

BOBBI DePORTER

Learning Forum Publications

Published by Learning Forum Publications

Submit all requests for reprinting to:
Learning Forum Publications
1938 Avenida del Oro
Oceanside, CA 92056
760-722-0072

Cover design by Greenleaf Book Group LP
Interior design and composition by Greenleaf Book Group LP

Library of Congress Control Number: 2006920933

ISBN-10: 0-9455253-8-9
ISBN-13: 978-0-9455253-8-7

Printed in the United States of America

08 07 06 10 9 8 7 6 5 4 3 2 1

To all of you who strive to attain and live Quantum Success.
To my partner and husband Joe Chapon, my children
Grant and Dana and my grandchildren Bryan, Sarah,
Hannah and Margo . . . you light up my life.

Contents

Quantum Success:

Quantum Success is the energy shift that occurs when
the 8 Key Catalysts and adaptability skills propel your
inner vision into dynamic focus.

Foreword

For me, the energy shift that propelled my vision into dynamic focus was the result of a series of fast-spinning life events that culminated in the summer of 1982 in the meadows of Lake Tahoe. My partners and I had just completed our first SuperCamp for kids. The premise of the camp was that every kid has a hidden genius; the goal of the camp, to help them bring it out.

On the first full day, the kids had walked in full of uncertainty. When they walked out ten days later, they were radiating joy, enthusiasm, and energy. They'd discovered themselves.

I remember one particular kid who came in very quiet and shy. He went through the whole experience slowly and hesitantly, and I felt the whole time as though I just couldn't get a read on him. Then, at the end, when we all gathered to make our farewell speeches, he got up and spoke to the entire group about how much the experience had done for him. He said it changed his life.

In that moment, everything snapped into clarity. I realized that my inner vision of helping kids discover their greatness, and the need I saw in the world had all come together—bam! I had become my vision, which made it possible for me to focus all my energies here and continue in this direction. From that day I had the sense that I was moving faster and faster in a direction that felt like what my life was all about.

Looking back twenty-five years, I attribute my achievements to living the 8 Key Catalysts that continue to propel me forward and make what I do meaningful and successful. This is my personal Quantum Success, and my goal in this book is to share its secrets with you.

Your ride to Quantum Success may begin with a sudden realization or a gradual series of Ahas. By mastering the 8 Key Catalysts and developing your adaptability, you too will carry your vision into the world with skill and joy.

I wrote this book to help you get there faster—to an amazing place of life fulfillment.

Bobbi DePorter, 2006

Acknowledgments

This book evolved like the process it describes. With clear focus I began with a plan, a discussion, and then a new plan, and on it went. I'm a believer in team and process . . . and I trust the dance.

What a truly marvelous, talented team supported this project. Direct, honest communication, putting ideas on the table, starting again . . . I feel very honored to have this support.

The ideas and story have accumulated over thirty years with so many wonderful, cherished people who have influenced my life and development.

A dear friend, SuperCamp parent, and supporter, DeeDee DeMan Williams, introduced me to someone she knew had the experience, talent, and vision to further ours. Sue Baechler "got" our vision—saw it, knew it, believed in it—and jumped in and has been supporting our direction to get what she believes is an important message out to the world.

Sue, in turn, introduced us to others. I'm honored to have the support of Ken Atchity, who I would best describe as director. He teaches through his directness, seeing what needs to happen and sharing his expertise. And Ken brought on others . . .

I'm very grateful for Julie Mooney's experienced and flowing writer's mind, and the patience and project supervision of Andrea McKeown of The Writer's Lifeline.

Clint Greenleaf was brought in to produce the book package and help us get it in your hands. It was a fitting, fun surprise when Clint and I remembered each other from the '80s—another successful SuperCamp graduate. I appreciate the caring work from Clint and his team at Greenleaf Book Group, in particular our project leader Lari Bishop.

I'm appreciative of all the wonderful, talented, supportive people I get to work with at QLN. Our SuperCamp Programs Manager Steve Arrowood was ready and willing to read through the text and comment on ideas to keep them true to who we are. Our facilitators and staff shared many stories that supported this book. We ride on the shoulders of all the people along SuperCamp's path . . . oh my goodness, so many . . . who have believed and given of themselves and their talent to further our vision.

Someone who greatly influenced my life's direction and vision is Marshall Thurber, my former partner at the Burklyn Business School. His vision, ideas, and teachings continue to inspire many. The business school lives on through the leadership of my long-time friend DC Cordova.

I thank my friends DC, Vishara Veda, Jerry Weinerth, Steve Curtis, and Bill Galt who supported me when I most needed it. You know the story.

I thank and acknowledge my SuperCamp cofounders, Eric Jensen and Greg Simmons. It was quite the exhilarating and exhausting ride of faith when we began. Thank you for the partnership that formed and launched our program.

My family has been truly supportive as I share the story that they lived. My children, Grant and Dana, my daughter-in-law Joanna and son-in-law Michael, and my grandchildren bring meaning and joy to the ebb and flow of life. I appreciate my sisters and our gatherings to share stories of our youth. In the memory of my mom, dad, and first husband, Don: I feel very blessed.

How wonderful to share a vision, purpose, and life with my partner and husband, Joe Chapon. You bring my life into dynamic focus and keep me grounded with your loving support.

And my thanks to a generous group of readers who committed to previewing the *Quantum Success* manuscript and sharing their feedback. Their collective imprint is in this book, and I acknowledge each of them by publishing their names in this first edition:

Randy Becraft, Nicole Bulone, Anne Bushong, Mary Dunn, Laura Forkner, Barbara Gee, Dan Jarmel, Jodi Johnson, Paul Kim, Annie Kim, John Klocke, Beth Moe, Patty McCullough, Alicia McManus, Colleen King Ney, Shushma Patel, Marianne Radtke.

Now it's in your hands—the readers I haven't met yet, but truly hope to hear from if this book has the impact on your lives that it has had for others. Enjoy!

Quantum Success

PART I

The Twenty-First Century
Is a Swirling Vortex of
Change—And This Book Is
Your Ticket to Ride

CHAPTER 1

What Is
Quantum Success?

When I learn something new—and it happens every day—
I feel a little more at home in this universe.
—Bill Moyers

Quantum Success is a term I coined to describe a phenomenon that takes place in people's lives when their personal interaction with the world transforms from energy into radiance.

I borrowed the word "quantum" that Albert Einstein brought to physics in the middle of the last century because the energy reaction that occurs in people's lives when they achieve Quantum Success is like the radiance he described at the atomic level. When these forces come together, they create a detonation. A profound transformation. A cosmic Aha.

Quantum Success is exponential. It lights up your life. It cannot be left at the office; it spills over into every aspect of your being. And it's the best way to shout back to the avalanche of chaos in modern life, because it is a *change-transcendent* success.

What brings people to this moment of radiance? It's a positioning. An attitude. It's about falling in love with yourself, your ability to learn, and your ability to transform the world. You have to work toward it by reaching inside yourself and living in harmony with that person moment-by-moment, answering to whatever life throws at you by adapting your knowledge and skills to serve your true mission in life. In sum, it's a personal vision, catalyzed by learning and life skills. It's vision-driven adaptability.

Most of the adaptability skills I introduce aren't new, and the Key Catalysts I promote have been around for millennia in the form of good old-fashioned character and smart living. But when you combine this adaptability with the anchor that these principles provide, and put them together with your own personal vision, they create an explosion!

Carry Your Vision into the World: Vision Cuts a Swath Through Chaos

Your vision is the overall direction in which your life is moving—the place where your values meet your deepest burning desires. It's the place where you perform the utmost service to humankind by being who you're truly meant to be. I am not talking about your goals, though goals play a part in your vision. It's not a destination, per se, because there's no end point for the journey, save death. It goes on as long as you do. Your vision gives a context to your journey—it gives the whole process a focal point. It's you as an engine, you as a rocket. It's you making a difference in the world by knowing yourself well enough to know the difference you're here to make.

Propel Your Vision: These 8 Key Catalysts Keep You Moving Forward

Quantum Success requires a coming together of all three elements. Vision without principles becomes ruthless. It can get so wrapped up in its own creation that it damages others, and in so doing, destroys its own mission, which is to serve. The 8 Key Catalysts, which you'll discover in Part Three, are to human life what gravity and the laws of matter are to the universe. They are the driving forces that propel our lives, and once you know how to harness them, they'll work for you.

These 8 Key Catalysts keep your journey true. In the midst of massive adaptation and knowledge acquisition, they help you remain focused on the *reasons* you're learning all this stuff. I use the term *Key Catalysts* to describe them because they are the "keys" to making our visions worth realizing, and the "catalysts" that turn random energy into directed energy, just as a propulsion system on a rocket takes an explosion and turns it into a launch.

Speed Your Ride: Adaptability Skills
Put You Light-Years Ahead

The third element in this explosive mix is adaptability. No matter how compelling your vision or how stalwart your character, you cannot realize much of your vision if you're not able to adapt to the realities of the world in which you're operating. The need for guided change and ongoing knowledge acquisition has always existed, but in the twenty-first century, it's vital.

The effective twenty-first-century person is a quantum learner, acquiring new knowledge quickly, deeply, and in many directions. Quantum learners process what they learn creatively, and can retrieve it an apply it in all kinds of new combinations. They are action-oriented: they learn in order to adapt.

Your Personal Aha: Quantum Success
Shifts Energy into Dynamic Focus

When these three elements come together, your energy changes. When all your energy is behind your clear vision, you have dynamic focus. You experience a transformation, a shift in the person you are. It's a shift in the way you learn, the way you live, and the way you interact with the people in your world. When this spontaneous "aha" happens to you, you become more creative, engaged, participatory, and enthusiastic. You'll experience success on a quantum level: meaningful success, whole-life success, change-transcendent success.

Here's the best news of all: you are capable of making this leap into radiance. You're probably far more adept at the mechanics of success than you realize—you've just never before marshaled all your success skills in this particular way. You don't need me to give you anything to make you a success; you already are one.

I've experienced Quantum Success for myself. I stumbled into it seemingly by accident, though nothing of this magnitude could ever truly be accidental. I'll begin with the story of my quantum discovery, then I'll devote the rest of the book to helping you discover yours.

CHAPTER 2

My Ride to
Quantum Success

My story of success may not be that different from yours. We've both faced challenges, hard times, defeats. But the fact that you've picked up this book is all the evidence you need that you're capable of Quantum Success.

What You'll Discover in This Chapter:

- Quantum Success: how I discovered it
- What Quantum Success will do for you

I am not a teacher. I am an awakener.
—*Robert Frost*

M̲y own launch to success began where it does for all of us: when I became conscious of that persistent voice inside my head that kept telling me I was meant to do something more. Following that voice took me from feeling like I was missing something to a sense of deep fulfillment—and from flat broke to international success.

Meant to Do Something More

I grew up in Seattle, Washington, one of three children. I was a shy kid with a quiet voice—I dreaded having to speak up in class. Like most shy kids, I had a tendency to become invisible. I behaved and maneuvered to avoid calling attention to myself. Even in kindergarten, I remember watching in horror when kids who misbehaved were sent to stand outside and wait in the hall. How embarrassing! I vowed to be good so that would never happen to me. My worst fear was of sticking out.

We lived on Lake Washington and played with a great group of neighborhood kids. We put on lots of plays and performances and enjoyed lots of lakeside parties organized by my mother. My love of celebration came from these parties, though I wouldn't make full use of it until much later.

I lived in the shadow of a talented older sister who was good at all sorts of things. In spite of my terror of "sticking out," I wanted to find ways to shine the way she did. In grade school, I decided to be an ice skating star. I remember practicing tirelessly at the rink, and overhearing my mother and one of her friends snickering in the stands. Although it was a brief reaction she thought I couldn't hear, it hurt; I remember it to this day. But then, I wasn't all that good at skating. I took piano lessons as well, and wasn't very good at that, either. My sister was great at it.

But for all my shyness, I was also gifted with a certain inner fire. I didn't let my fear of sticking out stop me. In fact, the pain my social awkwardness caused me made me acutely aware of other people who felt like outsiders. I did have friends, and I was so grateful to have them that I wanted to make sure other people had them, too. Whenever I noticed someone sitting alone, I'd seek her out and befriend her.

My teachers noticed my drive and initiative, and commented on it to my parents. In the sixth grade, to my astonishment, I was voted co-president of the student body. I remember the horror of getting up to give a speech in front of the students. My legs were shaking so badly, but I remained standing because I was determined to get through it. Years later, as an adult, I revisited my old grade school. I sat in the little seats, walked the halls, and visited the stage where I gave my first speech. In the intervening time, I had addressed audiences of thousands, yet when I stood in that spot, remembering, I could still feel that tremble in my legs all those years later.

After graduation and a little college, I married my high school sweetheart, whom I'd known since the age of twelve. Don DePorter was a charming up-and-coming hotel executive, and he and I both worked in my dad's hotel. I was nineteen.

Within a few short years, we had two wonderful children. When our kids were small, we lived in eastern Washington where the Columbia and Snake Rivers met, in a house that was near four others, and our five families became very close friends. We'd walk in and out of one another's houses at will. We'd often wake up to find our infant son wasn't in his crib—one of the neighbors would sneak in and take him over to her house to play, just so we could get a little extra sleep. We played jokes on one another. One night Don came home late and brought the hotel band with him. The band quietly set up in our neighbors' living room, and at precisely 3:00 AM, struck up a lively tune.

Marriage was what I wanted at that point in my life, and what all my friends were doing. The role of wife and mother was alluring, and was the norm at the time. It didn't occur to me that there were other choices. I was happy for a while—I adored my husband and children. I did love being involved in my kids' lives, and Don was supportive and fun to be with. I had a gratifying life as a young wife and mother. But something started growing inside me, a feeling of wanting to venture out into the world and do something more.

I noticed that my father, also in the hotel business, took far greater pains to teach the trade to my husband than he'd ever taken with me, although I'd been involved in the business too. I began to realize that nobody seemed to see the potential in me; nobody recognized that I could make a contribution beyond caring for my husband and family. I was a pleaser, there to support the dreams of others. I can't remember anybody asking me about my own dreams.

I had married very young, and the only dreams I had expressed were the ones that involved being a wife and mother, and my family *did* support me in those dreams. Part of having support for your dreams lies in expressing them so that people can support them. But no one encouraged me to do anything beyond my stated goals of wife and mother.

I became depressed and began searching for a way to fulfillment.

I applied for a job at Hawthorne/Stone, a local real estate firm. This company was a high-octane, success-bound place with a revolutionary attitude toward doing business. I wanted very much to work there, and when I walked in the door, it was with the intention of getting a job. I quietly held to the notion that I would be hired, no matter what happened.

The company partner who interviewed me made it clear to me what was expected. "Positive relationships with others are important. Always being open and growing is important. Results are important. You have to make thirty thousand dollars or more in commissions each year or you're not here."

I nodded. I believed I could do it. Some of the people there doubted my ability—even during my interview, I overheard one of the partners asking the man who hired me, "Why are you bringing in a housewife with no experience?" But I knew I wanted the job, so I simply didn't react to their doubts. Something about me made an impact on them. I got the job.

I crept in the door on my first day—it was a holiday, so no one else was there—and almost whispered into the phone to clients because I felt so self-conscious. That day, I made a contact that led to a sale worth thirty thousand dollars in commissions. My first day on the job, I covered my quota for the year.

Three years later, I made a deal worth eight hundred thousand dollars in profit shares and commissions, and over the next few years, I built a net worth of two million and became a junior partner.

I had an exciting time working there. I learned and grew. The atmosphere in that company was so joyful that it drew people. Even the mailman lingered after dropping off the mail each day, basking in the upbeat mood. The receptionist was always swamped with flowers because she received so much appreciation. It just felt so good to call in. The salespeople loved coming to work so much that they'd come in on their days off. We had to be forced to take time away. One day a month we had to stay out of the office entirely; they'd fine us if we showed up.

It was in this company that I learned the impact of environment. The right surroundings, the right energy in the atmosphere, can bring joy even to a repetitive task. I found myself bringing aspects of that environment home to share with my husband, kids, and friends. This new facet of my life added a layer of excitement and fulfillment to a life already filled with love and joy.

My family was supportive of this new chapter in my life. We hired a housekeeper to handle the household chores so that my time at home could be spent with my family.

Hawthorne/Stone ran on a win/win culture. The company only hired people who fit their vision, which gave the staff a deep sense of cohesion and belonging. It suited my gentle, soft-spoken nature. Here, my tendency to reach out to people worked beautifully because the company spirit was all about relationships and accountability. We were not only making a lot of money, we were also forging bonds and changing lives. I learned that if you have a vision, it's important to make it visible, to put it out where others can see it, to have everything about you speak who you are and what you stand for.

Within a span of four years, I'd gone from shy housewife to business executive.

It felt *great* to experience this success. It also changed the dynamics back at home. I remember sitting at dinner one night when my parents were visiting, talking excitedly to my dad about my job, while Don, who was into exotic cooking, discussed new dishes he'd created with my mom. Our housekeeper, overhearing our apparent role reversals, gave us a quizzical look. Don and I looked at each other and burst out laughing.

My experience at Hawthorne/Stone opened the door for a flood of success that followed. Because so many people were eager to work there, Marshall Thurber, a partner at Hawthorne/Stone, brought up the idea of creating a business school that would teach the principles that made it a success—a school where instructors could learn as much from the students as the students did from instructors, where learning was fluid and dynamic, success effortless, and relationships the center of everything. He and I discussed it at length, then we put together a plan and offered our first courses at a beautiful estate and country inn we purchased in Vermont. My husband and family were excited to see my vision become real. By 1978, the Burklyn Business School was off and running.

A massive inspiration and turning point for me, as well as the model for the teaching methods we use to this day, came from Bulgarian professor Dr. Georgi Lozanov. Although at the time he was largely undiscovered in this country, he created what is now known as accelerated learning. My business partner Marshall and I had heard of him, and when we learned that he was coming to the United States and planned to offer a workshop in the Washington, DC area, we tried to sign up immediately, only to find that the class was about to be canceled due to lack of enrollment. We couldn't let that happen. We called some friends, and we threw ourselves into getting the workshop to happen—we phoned people, spread the word, and hosted Dr. Lozanov in my home for three weeks. What we learned from Dr. Lozanov during this time transformed our work. I became deeply involved in the accelerated learning movement and remain involved to this day.

The second session of the Burklyn Business School incorporated many of his principles. Before long, many believed—including a professor who wrote business cases for the Harvard Business School—that our students were learning in six weeks what other business schools taught over two years.

It was about this time that my husband Don and I decided to end our marriage. I had come to see that I could no longer play the role that I'd taken on when I came into the marriage as a nineteen-year-old, and that his life lay along a different path than my own. We parted amicably and remained friends. I moved to a townhouse with our two children, although our son chose to live at our property in Vermont for a year to attend a wonderful one-room school there.

Shortly after that, the financial roller-coaster ride began. My business partner and I were trying to raise money for the school, and had gotten involved in the Chicago Board of Options as we were let in on an opportunity that we thought couldn't lose. A professor who taught for us told us about an investment method. We followed it on paper for the first six months. It worked great for those six months and for most of a year. We invested a little and made an enormous return. Then friends and associates started asking if they could invest with us. We were so confident about making money that we guaranteed their returns. And for a while, the system worked like magic.

Then, all at once, the bottom dropped out. We had brought so many investors in that we'd begun to influence the system itself. I watched in horror as my money dwindled away to nothing.

I lost almost everything—including our townhouse. Even our family's twelve-year-old Saint Bernard had to go. I remember shoving her into a car because she didn't want to go off to her new home on a family farm. Someone came into our house for a month just to sell our possessions. I remember thinking, as my memories were sold off one by one, if I just keep *this one thing*, I'll be okay—and then it, too, would be sold. We had this rare antique statue of a man that been a gift to our family—it had one arm broken off, but it was still considered valuable. I remember seeing a buyer walking out with the statue. I asked him how much he had paid for it, and he said the seller had let him have it for five dollars because it was broken.

But even with everything liquidated, I knew I'd never be able to repay all the money my partner and I had promised to our investors. I remember lying in a fetal position next to a telephone on the floor of a hotel room. I had to call one investor after another to tell them that their money was gone. It was so painful that I curled back into a ball on the floor between every call.

I remember feeling so alone. My partner became ill, and during this time I felt as though most of it was left to me to handle. It became necessary for my kids to move to Chicago to live with their dad. Some of my friends wouldn't even be near me during this time, as though failure and the pain I was going through were contagious and they didn't want to catch it from me. I remember packing up my remaining possessions into my car and wondering where to go. I recall dropping a few coins into a parking meter and thinking, *Well, this is all the home I've got, this parking space right here.*

One friend took me in and let me live in his lower floor apartment in Topanga Canyon outside Los Angeles. The apartment opened up onto a patio with a sparkling pool, and beyond, panoramic views. I spent some quiet time in this peaceful setting thinking and healing.

As painful as they were, my losses helped frame my future. Losing all my money made me realize I had gotten off track. At first the stock options system had served a purpose: to raise money for the school. But we'd gotten caught up in the moneymaking "game." Stock options in and of themselves added no value to the world; our only reason for being involved was to support the work that *did* add something of value.

It was a painful loss, but it helped me discover something. After I lost all my money, most of my possessions, and even a few of my friends, I still had myself. I could lose everything and still be okay. I'd survive. Today, I'm less afraid of losing, because I've lost it all before and I know I can get through it. Since I'm not afraid of loss, the fear of losing no longer has the power to cripple me. I don't take undue risks—I certainly don't want to lose—but I don't let fear of loss stop me from doing something worthwhile.

I survived, and so did the business school. Our associates wanted it to continue, so we formed a partnership of eight people. I remained involved with the school for several more years. It recently celebrated its twenty-fifth anniversary.

After my "crash" I rededicated myself to my vision and began thinking about what the next step in its development might be. My own professional success had come from loving my job and the work environment, and feeling as though who I was mattered deeply to the work I did—this was the heart of what we taught at our business school. People's lives changed when they began living according to who they really were. An associate suggested we try a program for youth patterned after the business school. I began to wonder what life might be like for people if they could get to that transformational experience earlier in life. What if we could help make it happen for kids?

I talked over this idea with two associates. We got excited about the notion that the business success our adult students enjoyed could translate into school success for kids. We could help great kids become even greater!

It wouldn't just be about learning new skills. It would be a life-changing experience. We wanted kids to discover the vast power within their own identities. If we could do that, they'd never again approach school—or anything else—the same way. Imagine if kids didn't have to cross that shaky bridge into adulthood with trepidation and frustration. What if they could charge into their teen years full of confidence and enthusiasm? The ennui would vanish, replaced by a passionate thirst for knowledge, experience, and growth. I had seen this happen with adults and wanted it for kids. And I came to see that this was a huge part of my contribution to society and it brought me a sense of fulfillment.

All at once I understood. I was here to help kids, to make this happen for them. That was my spark, my personal Aha. At that moment my own passion went quantum.

Youth and Learning Become My Dynamic Focus

The premise of SuperCamp was that every kid has a hidden genius; the goal of the camp: to help them find it and bring it out. The idea was that genius and magnificence would naturally surface when kids were immersed 24/7 in an atmosphere that supported it. On top of that, we'd help kids discover *how* to learn, not *what* to learn.

Though I had seen these kinds of transformations happen to adults, I wasn't sure if it would happen the same way for kids. I was determined to see if we could make it work.

I began making calls to friends, associates, and graduates of our business school (many of whom had said they wanted a similar experience for their children) and spreading the idea around. The concept took off almost immediately. We planned our very first SuperCamp for the upcoming summer. We funded the first camp on a shoestring. I found a banker who was willing to give me a loan on my car—he is still our banker twenty-four years later. I set up the camp's "office" on a card table in my bedroom. Everything fell together spontaneously. We even hand-colored parts of the brochures.

Parents loved the idea; their teens weren't too sure about it. At first suggestion, it seemed to them like something grownups were imposing on them, kind of like the broccoli that their parents made them eat. My son and daughter agreed to try it, but with hesitation: "This better be good, Mom." Involving them was a risk. If they didn't like it, they'd probably be less likely to try anything else I suggested in the future. I wanted them to like it.

We held our first SuperCamp in July of 1982 at Kirkwood Meadows around the Lake Tahoe area. We had sixty-four campers and a long waiting list. We were able to accomplish a lot in a short time because the kids were in an environment of excellence twenty-four hours a day for ten days. This first SuperCamp went beyond expectations and seemed to gain a life of its own. Listening to the closing sharing of the students, I knew we were on to something good. I particularly remember the youngest student, a small boy who never spoke in front of the group throughout the program. But on the last day, he stood in front of the entire camp and told us how much he had gotten out of the experience. At first there was silence, and then a thunderous applause, with students standing on tables yelling acknowledgements. I looked at him standing there, shyly taking it all in, and knew I wanted to focus my life in this direction.

SuperCamp snowballed from that first program. Our second year, we had four camps in different locations, and every year after that, it kept spreading. It wasn't all smooth sailing, but my passion for it was so strong that I kept charging ahead.

At about this time I married Joe Chapon, whom I had met and fallen in love with at the business school. He became deeply involved with SuperCamp. After the camp's first year, one partner left. Then, five years in, Joe and I bought out the other partner. Today he and I still operate SuperCamp as partners.

With SuperCamp's overwhelming national success, we began to think that what worked for kids in this country could work for kids in other countries as well. We started camps in Moscow, Singapore, and Hong Kong. Despite formidable cultural differences—a few of which we learned about the hard way—the experience of self-discovery and taking charge of one's success is so powerful that it transcends cultural boundaries.

Expanding My Vision into the World

A true vision is never fulfilled; as soon as one facet of it becomes realized, it expresses itself in expanding opportunities. With the success of SuperCamp, teachers and parents took note of the changes in their kids and asked us if the same things that energized kids could be made available to adults. Seven years into SuperCamp's success, we renamed our company Learning Forum. In addition to the camps for young people, we began to help teachers and leaders bring to the classroom and workplace the same transformations kids experienced at SuperCamp.

What began as a flashbulb in my head and developed on a shoestring has grown to international acclaim.

The ride didn't stop there, either. Recently, the Learning Forum has become the Quantum Learning Network—the umbrella name for our company. We have found that people of all ages want to become Quantum Learners to take their skills and attitudes to a higher level of effectiveness. Today, our products and methods are used worldwide—in classrooms, workshops, public seminars, and our camps—to create successful lives and effective learning cultures in schools, businesses and families.

Like all visions, the Quantum Learning Network is a work in progress, and there's always more to do. Recently, we began to look for a way to pull together all of our experiences into a single, powerful message, to boil down what we do to its bare essence so that we could apply it in the broadest possible context. We wanted to make the experience available in book form so that it could reach the public at large. When we mixed together the methods, life-truths, and spirit of what we teach, we were left with a vision of joyful, self-affirming, highly adaptable excellence. We called it Quantum Success.

This book will let you in on its secrets.

What Will Quantum Success Do For You?

Quantum Success brings about a shift in you as a person—a shift in focus, energy, and learning. You're more aware and awake in your life. You'll know your dreams and have the confidence to make them happen. One day, you'll discover you've become a freight train. Pure power. Unstoppable. You'll still be you. But you'll be exponentially *more* you than you've ever been before. You'll experience a more meaningful and joyful life by knowing who you are and being who you are.

What Quantum Success Will Do for You

- Quantum Success builds on the personal success you've already achieved.
- Quantum Success creates a shift in the way you live and learn.
- Quantum Success brings you to dynamic focus.

CHAPTER 3

You Are Capable of Quantum Success

You've got many of the tools you need to achieve
Quantum Success—you have a multitude of victories
under your belt already. Here you'll discover how to tap
into your own storehouse of success expertise to propel
yourself further down your personal path to fulfillment.

What You'll Discover in This Chapter:

- How to tap into the success that's already inside you
- How to win success by building on what you've
  already mastered
- How to create your own cosmic Aha
- What to expect in the chapters of this book

I am always doing things I can't do. That's how I get to do them.
—Pablo Picasso

You're an Old Hand at Success—and I Can Prove It

On Day Five of SuperCamp, campers go outside and rally around a wobbly thirty-foot pole with a tiny platform at the top. We tell them they've got to climb to the top of this pole, stand, and then jump off to grab a trapeze suspended six feet away. If they make it, they hang there for a moment, then they let go and are guided to the ground by teammates holding ropes. If they miss, the ropes still catch them and bring them down safely.

Campers are strapped into safety harnesses before their climb; they can't fall and injure themselves. But the harness does little to ease the sheer terror of heights that's built into almost all of us. That primal fear of falling is embedded deeply in our minds—perhaps even deeper than the fear of public speaking!

Whatever we have the students do, I do myself. I'm not normally afraid of heights, but the first time I did it, when it came time for me to jump, my legs wouldn't move. My mind said *Jump*, over and over, and nothing happened. Finally, with everyone watching and cheering me on, I jumped and caught the trapeze—and came down with a firsthand understanding of what it was like for the campers.

At every session, there are hesitant campers who say, "I can't do it!" These campers may tremble visibly, and some may even burst into tears. But the group rallies around them, calm, supportive, and confident.

"You can do it," campers and staff tell them—not even as encouragement; it's a simple statement of fact.

And they're right. The trembling kids make it up the pole, stand, and jump. And find out that they *can*. They learn that they're fully capable of doing something that terrifies them—something that, moments ago, they believed they'd never do. They discover that they can overcome it.

And they discover something more: if they can do that, they can do *anything they set their mind to.*

You may not have jumped off a pole, but you've done the equivalent. Throughout your life, you've been practicing the basic mechanics of success, whether you realized it or not, by learning how to do things you couldn't do before you tried.

Learning is pure magic. It's about achieving the seemingly impossible. What's impossible for you today can become possible for you tomorrow. All your life you've been making impossible things possible by your natural ability to learn and your built-in desire to explore.

> Sheryl Freedman, one of our facilitators, told me she once knew a bus driver who drove the same fixed route every day. He managed to take what might otherwise be a mundane job and turn it into something wondrous. Whenever a passenger would board his bus, he'd say, "Tell me you're somebody." Sometimes he'd shout it to the whole busload and they'd all shout back in unison, "I AM SOMEBODY!"

You don't have to wait for a special place or occasion to make a difference. Wherever you are, whatever you're doing, you can take it quantum.

Build on What You've Already Mastered

Quantum Success is about falling in love with your own ability to succeed. It's about realizing that you—just as you are—are capable of changing the world. When you realize the pure potential that resides in you, when you become aware of just how much you're capable of—*right now*—you can't help getting caught up in the excitement.

You're *already* a success. You may or may not have achieved the level or the type of success you envisioned. But either way you've succeeded beautifully in life—in more ways than you realize. No matter what dream you're chasing, you'll get there the same way you achieved everything else you didn't know how to do. You may already have achieved or come close to Quantum Success. You may have felt the energy that comes when you're close to being all of yourself.

What propelled your present accomplishments will carry you into the world at large—as far as you want to go.

Throughout this book, we're going to tap into what you already know about success, and use it to fuel your quantum ride to the meaningful life you've always envisioned.

Steve Jobs, CEO of Apple Computer and PIXAR, was fired from Apple when he was thirty years old. Of that experience, Steve said, "Something slowly began to dawn on me. I still loved what I did. The turn of events at Apple had not changed that one bit. I had been rejected, but I was still in love. And so I decided to start over. I didn't see it then, but it turned out that getting fired from Apple was the best thing that could have ever happened to me. The heaviness of being successful was replaced by the lightness of being a beginner again, less sure about everything. It freed me to enter one of the most creative periods of my life."

Quantum Success Puts You Back in the Pilot's Seat

Quantum Success isn't like other success books you've read. This time, you're going to remain in charge throughout the whole process.

Nobody can jump off the pole for you and give you the satisfaction of having jumped.

Many popular success and recovery programs expect you to turn over your free will, to put yourself in the experts' hands, to trust that they know what's best for you. This book is about you deciding what's best for you and taking the steps that fit with your goals.

There is no such thing as a generic, one-size-fits-all package of success. It can't be sold by the gross. It's unique for each one of us because we're unique.

I'll explain it this way: Quantum Success is you being fully yourself. It's "applied you." It's the radiant explosion that happens when you discover that your existence has a genuine, tangible purpose in this world, and when you move to fulfill that purpose.

> I'm passionate about youth and learning. It's what my life is about. People ask me when I plan to retire. Are you kidding? Joe and I just purchased a 42,000-square-foot building to expand our operations. I love to get excited about each new program, each new country, each new product. I live for every story from students and parents telling me how they've been touched.
>
> My joy comes from making a difference in people's lives by being who I am, from turning passion into action.

*There's nothing wrong with retirement
as long as it does not interfere with one's work.*
—*Benjamin Franklin*

Get Ready for a Quantum Shift!

Throughout this book, my goal is for you to experience that magical quantum shift in your being—that cosmic Aha. You've just completed Part One of the book, introducing you to Quantum Success and its creation. Since vision, Key Catalysts, and adaptability are the three vital elements of Quantum Success, Part Two will help you act on your personal vision. Part Three will introduce you to the 8 Key Catalysts that help propel your vision and keep it on track, and Part Four will provide you with the skills for developing adaptability, so that you create and respond to change in the course of your ride. Part Five will help you celebrate the joy of living your quantum success.

> At SuperCamp, we write one of our driving goals on one side of a one-inch-thick pine board, and our fears and doubts about reaching that goal on the other side. Then we break through these barriers to our goals by breaking through the boards with our bare hands.

> The first time I did it, my intention was really strong and focused and the board almost seemed to part before my hand. Before I did it, I thought it was impossible. Then I did it. My mind shifted. I felt a surge of power and thought, "If I can do this, what else do I think is impossible that I can do?" I started going over and over in my brain, looking for old assumptions to conquer.

> *Trust yourself. Create the kind of self that you will*
> *be happy to live with all your life.*
> —*Foster C. McClellan*

What You, Success Expert, *Already* Know About Success

- You've been mastering success with every personal achievement.
- Your quantum shift will happen when you discover the power you have to change the world because of who you are.

PART II

Carry Your Vision into the World

What's the single most important factor in your success? What one element is so vital to success that without it, all your best efforts can't possibly get you there?

You must be yourself.

At the heart of Quantum Success is identity. The kind of success you're seeking—the kind that plumbs the depths of your soul and manifests throughout your life—only comes from making a significant, positive contribution to the world by *being who you are*.

This idea is central to the work I do. SuperCamp works because it helps kids shift *their* energy into focus and recognize how great they are. When they realize they're liked for who they are, when they're being their authentic self, people automatically rise in their own esteem, and begin to see their own ability to make an impact on their world.

When you realize that Quantum Success isn't about denying your deepest drives but *throwing yourself into them headlong*, your life begins to change. Success demands a high level of self-awareness. You start down the path to Quantum Success by coming to the heart of who you are, by embracing your right to express yourself, and by discovering the powerful, calm self-confidence that comes from knowing yourself.

Many kids in school don't think they have the right to question the teacher. They doubt themselves and their capabilities. They think they're the problem. It's great when they discover that they're not only okay but *great*, and they have the right to express themselves and find their voice.

Shyness is really a mask. When I was a child, I often put on that mask. I didn't express myself because I was afraid I'd sound stupid and others would think badly of me. It was safer to stay quiet.

Adults struggle with this issue too. A person who yearns to live life as an artist won't speak of his passion to his best friend who thinks "doing creative stuff" should be confined to hobbies.

What does it take to just be who you are?

In the next four chapters, you and I are going to explore your inner vision—your view of who you are, what you're here to do, and why it matters. We're going to look at your values, your talents, and your desires. And we're going to put them all together and see where they're pointing you.

We'll also look at ways you become your vision: live it, model it, share it, exude it. And we'll discover ways to act on your vision by creating meaningful environments that reflect your vision and how to seek relationships with people who share your values and support your vision.

CHAPTER 4

Ignite Your Inner Vision

What's inner vision? It's the overall direction your life is moving. It's not a destination, but a direction, because as long as you're alive, you're never finished. As soon as one leg of your ride is completed, another one opens up before your feet. Your inner vision is what gives context to the ride—it's the reason behind each step you take.

What You'll Discover in This Chapter:

- The place where Quantum Success is born
- Why the world *needs* your inner vision
- Why it's better to risk seeking an inner vision than to play it safe as a "pleaser"

Vision abides . . . it is the only thing that abides.
    —*Miguel de Unamuno*

Vision, by definition, is a matter of the heart. It's the story of the love affair between you and the world. Inner vision is about acting from a belief that things can be even better than they are—and that you're somebody who can make them better.

Visions and dreams can be individual or shared: your unique inner vision directs your personal success; the dream you build with others in your group directs the success of the group as a whole. Vision makes the difference not only in businesses, but in families, community organizations, charitable foundations—in any group of individuals who are striving together toward a common goal.

Close-knit families and community groups have always known this, but the idea's been slow to trickle into the business world. Until the last few decades, many people assumed that matters of the heart didn't belong in business, which was about things that could be measured and exchanged. Today we're coming to understand that the most magnificent businesses are all about people and passions—even though the end product or service may still be measured and exchanged. A company can nurture personal growth and still succeed—in fact, doing so creates a far more meaningful success because it comes from *inner vision* instead of being imposed from outside. Any endeavor, whether a business venture, a group effort, or a personal quest, gets its power from *inner vision.*

Vision gives you a deeper reason for doing what you do. It adds meaning, purpose, and fulfillment. When something goes wrong, inner vision can keep you from giving up, because you're more committed to the journey than to the outcome of any one endeavor.

And when things go right, when something happens that rings a note in harmony with your inner vision, you get excited: "Yes! *That's* why I'm here!" When you operate from a strong sense of your own inner vision, you don't need to prop up your motivation with superficial rewards and external stimuli; your motivation runs deep and true because it's powered from within.

Vision gives what you do a context. Marshall Thurber, my partner in the business school, explains it like this: Imagine a bowl of fruit. The fruit is the content; the bowl is the context. The fruit is the outcome: your product, your service, the end result that you have to offer the world. The bowl holds the fruit in place; without it, the fruit would be scattered and lost. An endeavor is only as strong as its context. When the context is loose—in other words, when the bowl is weak—people are frustrated and the endeavor is inefficient and unproductive. When context is strong and well-defined, people are propelled by a sense of purpose.

Vision is what gives the whole context its cohesion. It's the shape these things form when you step back and view them all together.

Whatever your dream, context will likely be the bulk of where your efforts will be focused. Think of a rocket ship's payload. The cargo on board may be as little as 10 percent of what has to go up, but the other 90 percent (rocket fuel, frame, propulsion systems) is necessary to launch the cargo.

What is inner vision made of? The raw ingredients of inner vision are values, desires, and talents. But these ingredients alone are inert. Your inner vision only becomes activated when you see that your values, desires, and talents fulfill a need. Your passions and dreams graduate to inner vision status the day you put them into service for others.

Let's look at each of these three components of inner vision, then we'll look for ways that they fill a need in the world at large.

I created my company's vision with my husband Joe over twenty years ago. It feels amazing that after twenty years it's as powerful as it was when we first created it. To this day we use it as our guide:

An international model of excellence,
facilitating a shift in learning,
resulting in creative, educated, responsible people,
participating in the global community.

In other words, it's our way of changing the world. All our staff members know it. We go into it deeply, line by line. We look at what it means to us. It's the first thing I talk about when interviewing people for a position with us. My husband shares this vision and our dedication to supporting people in being lifelong learners and feeling great about themselves.

Your Values Drive Your Vision

An inner vision powerful enough to launch you into Quantum Success comes from your deepest-held values—even the ones you might not realize, or admit, that you hold.

What are values? Values are our subjective reactions to the world around us. They are like a weight we personally assign to our beliefs and interests.

Values are different from principles. Principles are laws of human interaction—honesty, integrity, commitment, and the like. Values are the things that are important to you—your beliefs, passions, priorities, causes, and even principles that you personally hold in high regard. Values are developed in childhood and shaped by culture, family, and experience. Values can change; principles don't.

When we're talking about your individual inner vision, we're talking about the sum total of values that drive you. When we're talking about the vision of an endeavor, we're talking about the values the members of the group hold in common. The individuals in a group don't have to have identical sets of values in order for the group to function, but they do have to have certain key values in common—the ones that are most important to them.

> Values are formed in part from our beliefs. For instance, SuperCamp was founded on the belief that all kids can succeed.

Let's begin by exploring your personal values. Write them down as they occur to you. Right off the bat, I'm sure you can name a dozen of your most cherished values. But even the most self-actualized person is always probing to discover what she values. Identifying values is an ongoing process because values can change, and because their influence can be so subtle that we may not realize for quite a while that they're affecting us. Or we may not be able to identify them accurately until some experience brings them to light.

In my company we dedicate time to discovering and clarifying our shared and personal values. Once a year we devote a full day to strengthening our vision. "Vision Day" is all about values. Families can do this too. So can you—you can devote a day to tuning in to the values that drive your personal inner vision.

Where do you look when you're trying to discover your values? Look at the values of friends you respect. Do you cultivate these values in yourself? Look at your heroes and teachers. What do you admire most in them?

> At SuperCamp we have an activity that encourages students to reflect on what they value, what they stand for, and how they show it. One by one they stand on an elevated platform on stage

and say "I am (full name). One thing I value in my life is ____
_____. I will show this by _____. Tonight I take a
stand for my greatness."

Every time I've done this myself, I'm reminded that what I
value is youth and learning. I show this with my commitment
to expanding our programs and to reach ever-growing numbers
of students. It's what I'm passionate about. It's what gives me a
great sense of fulfillment.

Look closely at your failures. Often, you'll find that your worst
mistakes happened because you failed to adhere to your own values. My stock option crisis taught me something vital about my
values. After a period of reflection, I came to see that I'd gotten
swept away by the moneymaking game, and had let my focus
slip away from what really mattered: helping people to learn. The
money was only a means to an end. My focus was still on helping people learn, but I justified my involvement in the options as
something that would support the good work that we were doing.
I was out of my area of expertise and had no business being there.
It was too far away from the core of my values.

Examining your values now may even help you avoid future
mistakes. If you take the time to discover what matters most to
you, you may not have to fail to find out. Knowing what's important can keep you from going down the wrong path.

Develop a system for checking in with your values. Make it a
regular habit and schedule it. Write your values down; post them
in your work and living spaces. It's very helpful to put your values
in writing. The written word gives them power.

Your values alone may not suggest a specific direction, but
they'll certainly put you in the right neighborhood. As you
work through potential applications for your life, you can check
them against what you value most and know instantly whether

or not a given direction serves your inner vision. Primatologist Jane Goodall had been in the business of studying African animals for many years when she found her true Aha. In 1986 she changed the focus of her life's work from research to advocacy, suddenly conscious of the "inexplicable instinct" to protect all living things.

Your Desires: What Are You Burning to Do?

I'm passionate about young people and learning. It's what my life is about. If I were living my life any other way, I'd be constantly fighting against the urge to work with young people in a learning environment, because that's where my desire is always pulling me.

What do you yearn for? What were you built to do?

Once when my company had a vision day, I set the mood by playing the upbeat song "Only If . . . (You Want To)" by Irish singer and composer Enya. In it, Enya sings, "If you really want to, you will find a way." Desire is a powerful obstacle-breaker. It can motivate us to break through seemingly insurmountable problems. It does this by the power of sheer momentum. Desire creates an impulse to move, to pursue.

Something happens when you begin to move toward what you love most. There's magic in that impulse—and in the movement itself. You can dream about it all you want, you can lust for it for years, but the universe doesn't change until you make that first step toward what you want most. Henry David Thoreau said, "If one advances confidently in the direction of his dreams, and endeavors to live the life which he has imagined, he will meet with a success unexpected in common hours." Once we give in to the urge to go after what we desire, the laws of the universe begin working in our favor. Once we're in motion, it almost becomes harder for us to *stop* moving toward our goal than for us to achieve it.

Give in to the urge to follow your desires, and you overcome the inertia that robs so many people of success.

In fact, chasing your desire is not only helpful, it's necessary to Quantum Success. In order to achieve Quantum Success, incorporate your desire into the picture, or else the thing you lust after will continue to steal your energy and sabotage your efforts. Think of all that wasted energy! It's like tugging against a giant magnet. No matter what you do in life, if you're resisting going in the direction life is trying to pull you, you'll *never* achieve the energy level you'd have by launching *toward* the thing you want most and letting the natural energy of the universe move you along. Where attention goes, energy flows.

Seek out the direction that makes you resonate. What draws you the most? Where is the energy greatest? Where is the area of maximum excitement? That's the place where your power to change the world resides. That's where you need to go.

When you launch yourself toward the thing you're meant to do, you'll experience both a tingle of excitement and a profound sense of calm. It's an Aha, but also an "ahhh." Your true path in life has a feeling of rightness to it. When you orient yourself toward your deepest desire, you'll feel as though your piece of the universal jigsaw puzzle is settling into place—right where it belongs.

You can put yourself onto the right path at any stage in your life, regardless of your age, regardless of how long you might have been on a path that really isn't "you." People start off on the wrong path for all kinds of reasons. College students are often influenced by parents in the choice of their major and their direction in life. They're unsure, so they take the advice.

My sister, who married and had children young, went back to get a degree in her forties. She had always wanted to be a doctor. When she spoke of it, our parents suggested she do something practical that takes less time to achieve, like accounting. But in spite of this pressure, she followed her dream and graduated from med school at the age of fifty. *Good Morning America* had her on the show to celebrate her achievement. After teaching and practicing medicine at the University of Southern California for a number of years, she now works with one of her sons, also a doctor, in her own private practice.

Your dream is who you are; it doesn't go away during your lifespan. What you're meant to be is what you're meant to be for as long as you're here.

Your Talents: Where Do You Shine?

Martin E.P. Seligman, author of *Authentic Happiness*, claims that every person has "signature strengths."

The happiest people know how to put their strengths to use. What do you bring to this ride to Quantum Success? What are you good at? What natural strengths do you have that predispose you to certain lifestyles, certain vocations?

Don't limit yourself to choosing only those things that you have a knack for; you're so adaptable that if there's a skill or learning method that you need in order to fulfill your inner vision, you can acquire it. But your greatest odds for Quantum Success lie along the path that utilizes what comes naturally—particularly in the beginning.

Just as you did with your values and desires, you get to know your talents by cultivating self-awareness.

> Bestselling author J.K. Rowling was on what was for her an unfulfilling career track for years, working as a secretary. The only thing she claimed to like about being a secretary was being able to type up stories on the computer during lulls in her work day. When at last she embraced story-writing as her focus in life, the rest, as they say, was history.

When I invite you to explore your talents, I'm not just talking about areas you're good in, like math or cooking, but the sum total of your strengths, including interpersonal skills. Even if you're terribly shy and socially awkward, you have more social competence than you realize. Whether or not you're great at sparking a conversation with a stranger, you may excel at hosting people; you might have a native ability to make guests feel comfortable. Even in areas that aren't generally your strong suit, you'll find places where you shine.

You'll be discovering and developing new talents all the time. But if you start off recognizing the areas where you're strong, and shape your inner vision initially from these points of strength, you're starting your ride to Quantum Success with your best foot forward.

> I bought the book *Now Discover Your Strengths* by Marcus Buckingham for our entire staff and my family. On our organization chart I added everyone's top five strengths. We had several meetings analyzing our strengths, asking questions like "Do all salespeople have the same or similar strengths?" and so on. People looked to see if they were using their strengths and also if their job required doing things that were toward the bottom of their list.

Supernova! When Your Values, Desires, and Talents Meet a Need

Oprah Winfrey said, "The best way to succeed is to discover what you love and then find a way to offer it to others in the form of a service" (*O Magazine*, September 2002).

Look at the sum total of your values, desires, and talents, and ask yourself who could benefit from what you have to offer. What problem could you fix, what wound could you heal, what gap could you fill with what's inside you? The real alchemy happens when you discover that the world has a need for exactly your combination of gifts!

Answering this question is not a one-time activity. There's no single answer to the question of how to apply yourself. It's a process that will continue throughout your lifetime. As you follow your inner vision, as you meet with success after success, you'll discover that there's always a new challenge for you to grow into.

Maria Montessori had early life successes as one of Italy's first female physicians. But it was her alertness to the needs of the children she was treating that revealed not a medical problem but a learning problem. This insight propelled Maria to transfer her life's work to perfecting a method of education that worked naturally with a child's way of learning—known today as the famous Montessori Method taught in Montessori Schools worldwide.

The most successful people who ever lived regularly weighed their abilities with their society's needs and sought new ways of reinventing themselves. The most successful organizations do exactly the same thing; in fact, the best of them *plan* for ongoing reinvention—and regularly seek new applications.

This habit of seeking new "self-applications" is like an ongoing science experiment. At Hawthorne/Stone, the revolutionary real estate company that galvanized my inner vision of what a company could be, we made experimentation a regular part of our work. Every week we'd try a new idea. There was no such thing as a stupid idea in that company. We'd give just about anything a try for one week. At the end of that week, we'd meet to evaluate how it did. If you think you'd be good in a particular application, give it a try.

Five Ways to Cultivate a Vision

1. Know your values so well that nothing can derail you from them.
2. Acknowledge your passion—and teach yourself to communicate it.
3. Begin from your strengths, but be willing to step out of your comfort zone.
4. Experiment with new ways to apply yourself.
5. Get feedback from others.

How will you know when you're following your inner vision? You'll know you're on the right track when your excitement keeps building, when the work you're doing and the life you're living keeps feeling righter and righter—even if you're struggling to make things happen, even when obstacles seem insurmountable, even when you meet with opposition.

That's why a strong inner vision is vital: because if you're following an inner visionary path, you may be opposed. Following an inner vision is often risky. It often means doing things other people are afraid to do. It may mean looking a little weird, even a little crazy, to those who can't see what you see. It means refusing to live up to others' expectations of you, if they're the wrong expectations. "The difference between myself and a madman," said Salvador Dali, "is that I am not mad."

A true inner vision is a vision of good purpose. If you're indulging a desire that hurts people, you're off track. That's not your true self. You weren't built to be a destructive force. The deepest, truest expression of you is in an inner vision that gives something wonderful to the world, something that's uniquely yours to give.

Living this way will have an impact on those around you. You'll inspire some, but you may offend others. You'll have to be prepared to stick to your inner vision even if other people don't approve.

You'll have to let go of other people's expectations of you. Because living up to the expectations of others is a guaranteed recipe for failure. If you're a pleaser, you're fitting yourself to someone else's mold, the antithesis of Quantum Success. Quantum Success is all about you being yourself out in the world; its premise is that the greatest thing you have to offer this universe is you.

What You Now Know About Vision Can Change the World

- Quantum Success is born from inner vision, not imposed from the outside.
- You bring a unique combination of values, desires, and talents to your inner vision.
- Your inner vision exists to locate the "fit" between what the world needs and what you have to offer.

CHAPTER 5

Be Your Vision

Be a model of your vision. Live it so people
can see what it is.

What You'll Discover in This Chapter:

- The deepest satisfaction in life comes from doing what you love to fulfill a need in others.
- Your vision remains constant, but the *expression* of it must always be growing and unfolding.

To spend life for something which outlasts it.
—William James

Aspiring novelists are taught "Show, don't tell." In other words, give us the experience in action, don't simply hand us a dry descriptive. Make it come to life for us. We teach kids at SuperCamp to show along with telling, to become better communicators by *doing*, by putting what they wish to communicate into action.

You are the vessel for your vision. In order to harness the energy of your vision in service to the world, you must live it.

The purpose behind my inner vision is to help people fall in love with learning by falling in love with themselves. My goal is to affect more people. My ongoing purpose, which I'm pursuing throughout my lifetime, is to fulfill that goal to the greatest extent possible by offering that vibrant self-discovery and love of learning to as many people in as many places as I can.

To clarify, I'll borrow a lesson from Buckminster Fuller, an inventor, thinker, and architect who has been compared to Leonardo da Vinci. I had the privilege of spending time with Bucky, as he is called. Bucky was fond of an analogy that, if he were reading this chapter, he might have offered for clarification:

"What's the purpose of a bee gathering nectar from a flower?"

Pollination, you might answer.

"But the bee isn't aware of pollination. The bee is there for the nectar."

But pollination happens because the bee is gathering nectar, you might argue.

"Exactly," Bucky would reply. "The bee's goal is to get the nectar, even though it fulfills a side purpose of pollination."

In a similar sense, the purpose of school should be education, not getting good grades. High grades are side effects students experience when they're learning; they're not the purpose itself. The purpose of pursuing your dream is the service you provide to the world. But what propels you into that pursuit is the rapture you experience when you're doing what you love.

It's all about your focus. You're pursuing your passion because it's your passion, but is it for a higher good? When we put something in motion by moving toward a goal, it causes other events and results. The more positive our purpose, the more likely that the pursuit of our passion will create positive side effects.

Check In with Your Vision

Putting a vision into action is an ongoing experiment that unfolds moment by moment. It requires you to become vigilant with yourself. Monitoring yourself isn't just about being in touch with your deepest drives and desires. It's also about recognizing what's behind the things you do and catching yourself when you do something that isn't motivated directly by your inner vision.

Check in with yourself regularly. Pay attention when you find yourself justifying an action. If you discover you're justifying, stop what you're doing. Step back and take the time to weigh your action against your inner vision. Are you on track?

See the Big Picture

Your inner vision generates motivation, but revisiting, honing, and reinventing the *expression* of your vision keeps your motivation going strong. Visions are like living organisms: they're either growing or dying; there's no such thing as a stable state. When we don't learn, we backslide; when our visions aren't expressed in action, they wither.

Never let your inner vision lose momentum. Practice continuous reflection to keep your vision active. Build into your schedule the time to step back and get a contemplative look at the big picture.

Push On into Uncharted Territory

Quantum Success requires you to keep pushing outward from the mundane and the known. Hanging out in the comfort zone is safe and secure. It's also boring. Everything's predictable: we know what to expect; we've done it before. There's no challenge. That means there's no room for growth.

If you've ever been to a gym, you know that in order to get stronger you need to lift weights that are a bit heavier than the ones you're used to. If you want to keep gaining muscle strength, you've got to keep adding more weight. Likewise, your inner vision can't stay healthy unless you keep putting new growth challenges before it.

Quantum Success requires you to live in a perpetual state of learning. Learning only takes place *outside* the comfort zone—in what we call the learning zone. It's a challenge to step out, but then, aren't challenge and growth the antithesis of boredom?

Try new solutions; consider alternatives. Stand your problems on their heads. Seek out new ways of looking at things. Never let yourself get too satisfied or too comfortable.

Visions Transform from Ideas into Action

- Seek new ways to express your vision and to put it into action in service to others.
- Blast out of your comfort zone, stand old assumptions on their heads, and push out into uncharted territories.

CHAPTER 6

Reflect Your Vision in Your Environment

Your outside environment is a mirror of your inside environment. Environments affect your mood, thought, and focus, and reflect the person you are and the values you hold.

What You'll Discover in This Chapter:

- Your physical space can be an expression of your vision
- Environments can nurture relationships

Great things are not done by impulse,
but by a series of small things brought together.
—*Vincent Van Gogh*

You're an extraordinary person building an extraordinary life. You're breaking new ground and beating impossible odds. Since you're going after your dream, you owe it to yourself to do all that you can to assist your own efforts. Arranging your physical "outer" space to match your mental, emotional, and spiritual "inner" space is yet another way to bring all parts of your life in line—to make every aspect of your being speak the same message.

Little details make a big impact. Dr. Georgi Lozanov, father of accelerated learning and one of my personal mentors, says, "Everything speaks!" Your physical and emotional environment greatly impacts the quality of your life and work. Dr. Lozanov called his method "suggestology" because it was built on the premise that everything makes a suggestion—even when you don't receive its message consciously.

Space speaks. The more you become aware of its impact, the more you'll discover the subtle messages it's giving you. And the more you learn to listen to yourself, the more you'll know how to arrange your space to give you what you need.

Details make the difference. It's about tiny, subtle details that have a massive cumulative impact over time. I'm not the only one to advocate creating a nurturing environment. Whole branches of psychology, architecture, and the healing arts have been devoted to the effect of the physical world on our inner lives. The ancient Chinese art of Feng Shui, which has traveled through many cultural traditions and is currently enjoying popularity in the United States, recommends that environments be arranged to create a smooth flow of "life energy." The most uplifting, peaceful, and nurturing environments are clean, organized, and well-lit, filled with plants and colors. The effect is subtle but profound.

In the process of designing our new headquarters, I talked with a Feng Shui consultant. I'm very interested in the light, flow, and movement of the space. When I meet with our architect and look at the plans I can feel what it will be like to walk the halls, interact with people, and experience the light and space. When he comes back with revisions, the first thing I do is draw arrows from all the windows and skylights to see where the light will hit.

When our architect suggested a partition that would have solved one of the space problems we were facing, I vetoed it as soon as I realized that particular configuration would block the natural light to five people's workspaces.

Align Your Home and Workspace with Your Vision

Arrange your physical environments to encourage your dream. In the beginning days of SuperCamp my "office" was a card table at the end of my bed. It was all the new space I needed to speak my dream. With a little creativity, you can design spaces that remind you of who you are, convince you that what you're doing is wonderful, and boost your confidence in your ability to do it. Everything in the space can suit the purpose, support the atmosphere, reflect your values and nurture your spirit.

In my home, my favorite room has windows on all three sides and sliding doors that open onto our patio. I like to put a card table in the middle of the room and work from there. I love this space.

Create spaces that reflect your values. Decorate with objects and images that remind you of the big picture. Place them anywhere that feels right to you and uplifts you. You could even use them to frame your bathroom mirror, since gazing at an image of yourself while reviewing them will reinforce the message.

A friend of mine, Helice Bridges, has a program called Blue Ribbon Difference Makers. They have ribbons printed with "Who I Am Makes a Difference." She gave me a ribbon that I stuck on the inside of my bathroom mirror. When I open the cabinet each morning, I see it.

The act of taking care of your space is itself an expression of your vision. You can see it and feel it. It impacts all your senses. When your environment is the living embodiment of your dream, it's a lot easier to believe your dream is possible.

> Wherever we have training sessions, we rearrange the space to suit the need of the moment. When a hotel conference room we're using is bare, we roam the halls for objects we can use to create the environment we need. We'll borrow chairs, lamps, and plants from the lobby. Even when a space looks good, we're always seeking ways to make it better: "What more can we do?"

Arrange Your Space to Nurture Yourself and Others

At home, at work, and in all the spaces you inhabit, your physical environment can reflect the fact that people are central to your life. Design your spaces to nurture yourself and the people who matter to you, and to call forth in them those qualities you want to promote. Create spaces where you live and work that are designed to foster learning, creativity, and quiet reflection, and areas where family and friends can go to regain energy, refocus, and connect.

Living things bring a nourishing energy of their own to the places they inhabit. Sometimes taking care of others is the best way to take care of yourself. Add live plants, flowers, and if your lifestyle allows it, animals to your space. A couple of staff members who travel a lot have fish, since other animals aren't practical. When they travel they bring their fish to the office so coworkers can look after them. One staffer now keeps a fish on her desk at all times. One Fourth of July I stopped by the office to catch up on work and found a huge note on my desk: "Please feed Sue's fish. Place eight pellets gently on the water so they will float." This on top of the priorities I had made me smile.

On a recent trip to the Dominican Republic, Joe and I checked into a hotel room to find a round vase of water with what I thought was a single brown leaf floating in it. At first I thought, *That's nice that the hotel provides a flower vase; too bad they forgot to put in the flowers.* The next morning, I looked at the leaf and thought I saw movement. Joe said, "Yeah, that's a fish in there!" The hotel had provided us with a fish.

Your environment serves many purposes. Is yours conducive to creativity? Does your environment facilitate bringing people together? At Quantum Learning Network we have an annual Office Beautification Day, in which everyone cleans, renews, and redecorates their workspaces. It's a great team-building activity, one that works equally well for families, faith organizations, and clubs.

Your environment can also serve to remind you of your inner vision. It can be arranged and decorated to reinforce a message, goal, or concept. When hundreds of details converge to speak a single message, the message hits home. You can designate a wall in your hallway as a "success wall" and place portraits of people you admire, or put up a corkboard where you can pin quotations that inspire you. Let your spaces be *your* spaces.

Reveal your true nature to yourself with the objects you place on walls, desks, and tabletops. I travel abroad regularly to countries where our programs are offered. People in these countries have given me a number of cultural gifts and thank-you plaques on my visits. I display them on a special shelf in my office. As I gaze at each item, I relive wonderful memories.

Listen to yourself; take the time to understand the unique energies you need from your environment. Then create an environment that provides those energies. When you enter your spaces, imagine you're looking into a mirror that reveals your true self. Don't arrange your space according to who you think you are now, but according to *the person you wish to become*. Let your environment pull you toward the highest expression of yourself.

Your Physical Spaces Foster Quantum Success

- Listen to yourself and recognize what you need from your environment.
- Make your environment a mirror of your highest self.
- Arrange your spaces to nurture relationships.

CHAPTER 7

Seek Relationships That Support Your Vision

Quantum relationships are radiant relationships.
How much focus and intention do you invest in your
connection to the people who matter to you?

What You'll Discover in This Chapter:

- How to seek, hold, and treasure relationships with the people who matter
- How to surround yourself with the people who support you

A relationship, I think, is like a shark, you know?
It has to constantly move forward or it dies.
—*Woody Allen*

Relationships are among the keys to your success. All the other aspects of success can be taken away from you, sometimes by sheer misfortune. I found that out the hard way. But the two things that endure for as long as you're alive, no matter what your fortune or circumstances, are your identity and your connection to the people who matter to you.

I'll be using the phrase "people who matter" a lot in this chapter—who are these people? I'm not just talking about your closest friends, your family members, and the people who sit next to you at work. I'm talking about anybody with whom you interact in the course of living out your dream. When you look at relationships through that lens, no connection is insignificant. Your life is composed of all kinds and levels of relationships, from the most personal to the purely professional. Whether you're part of a group of two or a group of ten thousand, your success is determined by the quality of your connection to the people who matter.

When we put our time into relationships that support and nurture us, no other investment we can make brings a more satisfying reward.

Once I drew a sort of map of my relationships with branches for immediate family, extended family, and friends, with connections between different groups and events, just so I could get an overview of the way they all fit together.

I spend varying amounts of time with people. My husband is number one. My children and grandchildren are at the top of my list. But it's not about amount of time spent. I spend the most time with the people at my office, as it's the team that shares my vision and I'm there a lot. I have a best friend with whom I spend very little time, yet I know she loves me and she knows I love her. The balance in relationships is more about priority than it is a function of time and space. You don't need to make every relationship a top priority, but take time to reflect on the importance of each relationship and the sense of balance you feel regarding each relationship.

The importance of the relationship is also a function of the circumstance that brings the people together. You may have a very intense relationship with a group of coworkers during a project, with a deep need to nurture those relationships for that time. Then, when the project is completed, you may "let go." Movie actors often remark that the deeply emotional friendships they forge during filmmaking seldom seem to last—at least with the intensity they had when the project was active. On the other hand, the relationships of married partners carry an explicit permanence. Joe and I love to spend time together, but we're often apart, traveling. In our busy summer season, we travel in opposite directions to cover more ground. But even when we've been in the same office together all day, we still come home to sit on our patio and talk. We never run out of things we want to share. Our personal and professional lives meld together.

Meaningful Relationships Come from Common Visions and Values

What are great relationships made of?

People often form superficial bonds over shared interests: golf, aviation, horses, needlepoint, politics. Shared interests make for great starting points, but they're not the same as focus, intention, and shared values, the heart of meaningful relationships.

Individuals are frequently thrown together by accident. They end up sharing an office, a dorm room at college, or a place on the same committee. They may develop a passable rapport simply because of their shared circumstance. They may get along fine. But this doesn't make for a powerful bond, either. Strong bonds run deeper.

Some of the world's most successful dating services don't match people based on hobbies or careers. They match them according to deeply held values. The best marriages are made of such bonds. So are the best relationships of any other kind.

If you want to make the most meaningful connections to people, this is the place to do it. Seek out the places where your values and visions intersect.

Not your ordinary cocktail-party conversation, you say? It's true that a discussion of values doesn't come naturally to most people. Some even feel threatened when faced with the task of revealing such things. You do need to know who you're sharing with and whether it's appropriate. You wouldn't share your deepest feelings with everyone. But when you create an atmosphere that welcomes these revelations, you create a tremendous opportunity for people to bond on a profound level.

A friend of mine, Barbara Metzler, loves to get friends together and mix interesting people. At her dinner parties she will often pose a question and encourage everyone to answer. Recently at one of her dinners, she asked each of us to answer what we thought was the key to our success. I told the group about the 8 Key Catalysts and holding my intention for what I wanted to have happen. Others talked of going a step further than they thought they'd go. I felt I got to know the other guests on a much more profound level, and I will feel connected the next time I see them. Getting to know people at the level of deeply held values made for a meaningful evening.

At my company we use a slightly more formal way to get to know one another, one that you can adapt to suit your purposes. It works great in a business setting, but it could work equally well at a family reunion, a club rally, or a planning meeting. I know of someone who used it in conversation with someone he met on a train. That person became his wife a year later.

It's called the Affinity Exercise. I first learned it from a friend, Maggie Weiss. Here's how it goes:

Have everyone choose a partner. Have one person in each pair respond to these statements.

1. Tell me something I don't know about you.
2. Tell me something you like about me.
3. Tell me something we have in common.

In response to these answers, the person doing the asking says only, "Thank you." Since this single phrase is the response to their revelation, the partner can't read anything into the asker's reaction. When using this at home, you might let it spark conversation instead of just saying thank you.

First one person asks and the other answers, then they switch. And after the second round, they switch again. That's right: The same pair of people asks each other the same questions three times. Why is this? Because the first time around, people may be nervous, uncomfortable, and they don't express what's really meaningful to them. Often, something happens during that third round. That's when the trust starts to build and more meaningful responses pop out. *Then* we change partners.

The value of this exercise is the focus and intention it lends to developing relationships. It gives people an automatic structure to talk on a more intimate level. It gives them permission. It strips away the awkwardness and reluctance to talk this way to virtual strangers.

The Affinity Exercise is a magical process. The most remarkable things come to light. People who've worked side by side for years have discovered common interests. Almost everyone feels a closer bond. There's no downside to people in a group feeling closer to one another. And the positives are limitless.

When I interview people for a position, I talk about our vision and explain that we only want people to join us who share that vision. We continually keep our vision in front of us. We're all aligned around it and committed to it because we want to be.

Group members need not have met and interacted before to experience a strong bond with one another. Have you ever observed what happens when two Marines meet? An understanding passes between them. Even people meeting for the first time can come up with an answer to the question, "What do we have in common?" just by the fact that they're at the same gathering.

At our weekly meetings we have a different person each week get up and give a five-minute bio so that everyone can get to know that staff member better. Building strong relationships is an ongoing process. I used to think we could focus and work hard at building great relationships, and then go back to our "real" work. I quickly learned that as soon as you take your focus off building good relationships, they deteriorate.

Quantum Love Notes

Everyone likes to be reminded that they're appreciated. At SuperCamp, written communication that shows you're appreciated is a "love note." There's a board for love notes at camp for students and staff to express their appreciation or to acknowledge each other for something. Kids also write letters to their parents. They write not only about how much they love and appreciate them, but also apologies and lists of things they wish their parents knew about them.

Create a space for notes of appreciation in the places you share with others. It's a wonderful tradition for families. Get in the habit of writing little notes to people or sending them emails. When I'm going out of town I sometimes leave Joe a note where I know he'll find it.

Set a Check-in Time

In my company, we meet every morning for five to ten minutes. During that time we stand in a circle. The agenda is Reports from the Field (so we can keep connected with those of us who are traveling), FYI (what others need to know) and Burning Shares (things we're excited about, whether business or personal). This meeting helps us stay connected. Everybody has a chance to speak, and we take turns running the meeting. The structure of the daily check-in is itself an expression of our values.

Any group can develop the habit of a regular check-in. Families can pick a natural gathering time like dinner to hold their check-ins. One family I know starts each night's dinner conversation with, "What did you learn today?" Another family opens with, "What were the best and worst parts of your day?"

Clubs and civic groups can open their meetings with a check-in. Even friends can create a form of it to keep the relationship strong. Think of your closest friends—you probably do this informally, anyway. Do you call a good friend on Sunday evening just to see how his week went? Do you drop a line to your college roommate at Christmas and Easter? Keeping the contact regular, the topic open, and the discussion positive is key to keeping the relationship strong.

Welcome Newcomers

It's tough being new. When people enter a new group, they know little about how the group functions. Almost everyone wants to be included, but few people entering a new situation know how to fit in right off the bat.

In my company, we've brought a large group of new employees aboard and celebrated their arrival with a potluck luncheon. We set everybody the task of asking at least one of the newcomers one of three questions:

1. What's your favorite animal at the zoo?
2. What's your favorite movie? Why?
3. What's your dream vacation?

The conversations that came out of these questions were terrific ice-breakers. They created a great starting point for relationships that were forged over the months and years that followed.

We've also paired up and interviewed each other. The interviewer later shares the interview with the larger group. In addition, we write up bios given in our weekly meetings and have a booklet collection of these that new people can read.

When you make new people feel welcome and included from the beginning, you set the tone for their membership. Good things happen when people understand from the beginning that in this group, relationships matter.

Give Right-of-way to Relationships

Your success is built on strong relationships. Your dreams and passions might be the material your success is made of; your ambition, courage, and dedication might be the fuel that makes it go, but your relationships hold the entire rocket ship together. And they make the ride worthwhile in the end.

In my personal life and in my company, I place a high value on relationships. Valuing relationships doesn't mean sacrificing all to them; instead, it means evaluating each situation. I examine the needs of the project and the situation, along with my own needs and the needs of others, all under the microscope of putting a high value on relationships.

Building powerful relationships takes focus and intent, but if you invest in them, you'll receive ten times your investment in return.

Deep, Strong, and Meaningful Relationships

- You surround yourself with people who support you.
- You seek out common visions and values.
- You take time to check in with the people who matter to you.
- You seek, hold, and treasure the relationships that are important to you.

PART III

Propel Your Vision: 8 Key Catalysts

Every spaceship has a guidance system. You don't just strap tons of combustible fuel to a rocket, point it in roughly the right direction, light a match, and let it rip. You carefully build a system for controlling the ship in flight, for keeping the awesome combustibility that powers it from ripping it to pieces.

Your vision—to make it as dynamic as a rocket—needs a guidance system, too.

Enter the 8 Key Catalysts.

There's a reason I call these concepts *Key Catalysts*. In physical and chemical reactions, catalysts boost desired changes. In mental reactions, catalysts function just like keys in locks. Locks are designed to keep you out. When you're locked outside these concepts, you can't have access to Quantum Success. You can't succeed without them. To get to the magical catalytic reaction they offer, you have to grab hold of the keys and let yourself in.

We first developed the 8 Key Catalysts for SuperCamp, where they've been known simply as "8 Keys of Excellence" for the past twenty-five years.

In this book, you'll get to know these 8 Key Catalysts:

- Live What You Value
- Failure Leads to Success

- Speak with Good Purpose
- This Is It
- Commit Yourself
- Take Ownership
- Stay Flexible
- Keep Your Balance

Why can't you succeed without these Key Catalysts? Let's take a look at what your vision would look like without the catalysts to direct it. You want to achieve your dreams—you want it badly. But do you want it so badly that you'd use and hurt others in order to achieve them?

Isn't the whole point of pursuing your vision to do something good in this world with who you are?

If you're leaving a trail of disappointment, distrust, and pain in your wake, why does it even matter whether you reach your goal? Vision without principles becomes ruthless ambition. Ambition becomes so obsessed with itself that it doesn't care who it runs over to get what it wants.

You can't succeed in a life-supporting way without the 8 Key Catalysts because all eight serve relationships. They govern the way you interact with life, yourself, and others. These Key Catalysts are larger than time and place. They transcend culture and history. They're about as close as you can get to a universal human code of behavior.

In the next eight chapters, we'll explore these Key Catalysts one at a time: what they mean, why they're important, and how to make sure they're an active part of your vision.

CHAPTER 8

Key Catalyst:
Live What You Value

Live in integrity: conduct yourself in the state of
authenticity, sincerity, and wholeness that results when
your values and behaviors are aligned.

What You'll Discover in This Chapter:

- The litmus test for whether you're living a life of integrity
- How to show people you're trustworthy
- How to be loved for who you truly are

Integrity simply means not violating one's own identity.
—Erich Fromm

Quantum Success begins with knowing yourself: your values, desires, talents, and dreams. Integrity is all about being true to that self, in all your actions and interactions. This time, I'm not just talking about values and desires, but also about personality, preferences, opinions—all the factors that compel you to act and feel one way when another person might act and feel differently. Here's the take-away definition: integrity is *behavior congruent with your values.*

Remember geometry class? Remember learning about congruent triangles, with matching proportions? When you live with integrity, your values are in proportion with your actions, just like congruent triangles are proportionate to each other.

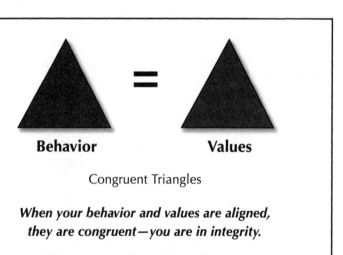

Behavior   **Values**

Congruent Triangles

When your behavior and values are aligned,
they are congruent—you are in integrity.

Inherent in the Key Catalysts is a universal code of human behavior. It's all about respect for the needs, rights, and freedoms of others.

At SuperCamp, we used to ask kids, "If I value money, is it okay for me to rob a bank?"

Living your values doesn't mean living selfishly or self-righteously, defensively claiming, "I have a right to be this way." At the extreme end of this continuum, a person could border on the pathological: "This is what I value: *only me.*"

Living your values doesn't mean harming, denigrating, or avoiding those whose values don't match yours.

There's a line of behavior that must not be crossed even in the name of values. Terrorists, for instance, cross that line. It doesn't matter that their behaviors are in line with their values. They're pursuing those values at the expense of other people.

Whenever the pursuit of values tears other people down, it's on the wrong side of that line. That's not our definition of integrity.

Take a moment and think about what you value. You might want to write a list. Living with integrity often amounts to choosing between short- and long-term benefits. It can mean sacrificing what you want now for what you want most, which is the reason it can at times be challenging to maintain. It requires living with a high sense of awareness, keeping your focus on your values at all times. For instance, let's say the two things you value most in life are your family and your career as an aspiring novelist. You burn to throw yourself into your writing career, but if your children are young, you know you can't do that. They need you even more than your writing needs you. And if you abandon them in order to write, what can you possibly write that will make up for the time away from your kids? Integrity is also about honoring your values in the right doses, with the right priorities. The best choice at any given time depends on your situation, and it is always unique to you.

Why Live What You Value?

When you act from your true desires, beliefs, values, feelings, and motivations, instead of disguising them or pretending they're really something else, you give the people around you the opportunity to see you. You're showing the world how you *are* instead of how you'd like to *look*. You're giving up trying to manage people's opinions of you. The reward you get in return for choosing integrity is that people will know you for your sincerity and honesty.

Integrity fosters trust and respect, the cornerstones of great relationships. Since great relationships are necessary to Quantum Success, you can't get there without integrity.

Integrity leads to fulfillment. Some of the first students at the Burklyn Business School were already millionaires, a status synonymous with success in many people's minds. But at the end of the school session, these millionaires said they'd found a new level of meaning and fulfillment, and the courage to follow their hearts.

Why Integrity?

- Integrity fosters trust.
- Trust is the foundation of relationships.
- Relationships are vital to success in all aspects of life.

Block Out the Noise and Pave Your Own Road—Guided by What Lights You Up

"Follow your heart" turns out to be the phrase most often spoken as the integrity ingredient for successful work and life journeys. After more than four hundred interviews with eighty-six luminaries (like Michael Dell, Sandra Day O'Connor, and Starbucks founder Howard Schultz) Road Trip Nation founders and followers have discovered that the common recipe for life success is figuring out what lights you up and designing work and life around it (www.roadtripnation.com). "What blows my mind is, most people say they don't know what they're passionate about," says one of the three Road Trip founders, Mike Marriner. In a *Fast Company* magazine article, ("Inspiration Junkies" by Danielle Sacks, Issue #100, Nov. 2005, page 95) Mariner argues that many actually do know what excites them, but lack the confidence to pursue their vision. Others are programmed to think their passions don't fit inside the boxes presented them in dusty college career centers.

What Does Your Behavior Say About You?

For this next section, you may want to jot down a few things. You'll need a pen and paper. If you don't have them handy, get them now.

Start by writing down five things that happened recently—the first five interactions with people that come to mind.

Now imagine you're looking at yourself doing these things. What do your actions say about you? If you find self-evaluation difficult, then pretend you're looking at someone else's five interactions—a stranger's, or those of a person you admire. What would you assume about the values of the person doing those actions? Make a list. Write down the values that those behaviors project.

Are those your values?

Now let's try a different exercise. Earlier, I suggested you make a list of your values. Consider making a chart of yesterday, writing down what you were doing. You can check them against your list of values.

Does your time go to the people and activities you value, or elsewhere?

These check-in exercises are the litmus tests of integrity. If your behaviors reflect your values, if your time goes to the people and activities that are most important to you, then you're living with integrity. If your time is disproportionate to your values, and your behaviors are saying things about you that aren't true—even if they're more flattering than the truth—then you're not living your life with integrity.

> Living in integrity means being true to who you are. My dad was a great example of what it means to be this way. He was at home in his own skin. He never struggled with public speaking the way I did. Before he addressed an audience I used to ask, "Aren't you nervous?"
>
> He'd reply, "Why would I be nervous?"
>
> He was always just himself.

How to Act with Integrity, Moment by Moment

A lot of people simply act as they feel like acting, then find some justification—any justification—for why they did what they did. Their actions are largely unconsidered.

Highly successful people, in contrast, use their values to steer their actions. They reflect, *then* act. Their values motivate their actions, because they choose their actions to harmonize with their values.

Check your motivations—can you be honest enough with yourself to really admit why you're doing something? Is it really a reflection of your values, or a reflection of what you want at the moment?

When I lost all my money—and other people's money—in the options investment strategy we joined to raise funds for the school, it would have been easier for me to shirk responsibility, justifying to myself and others that these people asked me to take their money. It was excruciating to make those calls and take the blame. But facing that responsibility was what led me to discover that I could lose nearly everything and still be me.

When Your Behaviors Match Your Values

Choose your behavior to reflect your values, and you'll move through life with authenticity, sincerity, and wholeness.

Remember the congruent triangles? Remember how balanced and solid they looked, how harmonious they felt? That's how your life will feel when your behavior is in line with your values.

When you live with integrity, it'll show. People will trust you, almost instinctively. They'll think of you as a person of your word. You'll be known for your strong character.

When you live with integrity, you'll enjoy a clear conscience. You'll be filled with good feelings about yourself. Those good feelings will pour into everything you say and do.

Live Your Life with Integrity

- Integrity is a necessary ingredient of trust, reliability, and strength of character.
- You can't have deep, solid, meaningful relationships without it.
- It's the only way people can know you and love you for who you really are.

CHAPTER 9

Key Catalyst: Failure Leads to Success

Failures provide us with the information we need to
learn so that we can succeed.

What You'll Discover in This Chapter:

- How to overcome your fear of failure
- How to fail less and succeed more
- How to keep failure from ever sapping your energy again

Experience is simply the name we give to our mistakes.
—*Oscar Wilde*

I f I say the word "failure," what emotion does it evoke in you? Guilt? Shame? Inadequacy? Not a pretty picture.

Failure is the label we stick on unsuccessful ventures. It's practically synonymous with incompetence. The word alone brings up feelings of shame and humiliation.

When we fail, we automatically send ourselves bad messages. We discourage ourselves from trying again, because if we try we risk another failure.

It's true that when you give up trying, you don't have to face failure anymore. But you'll have close to zero chance of achieving Quantum Success. To get there, you've got to be willing to fall on your face a few times.

You didn't start out hating to fail. When you were tiny, failure didn't weigh you down with emotional sludge. When you failed as a toddler, you had a good cry, then you stood up, dusted yourself off, and kept on going. But somewhere along the way you learned that trying and not succeeding was bad. That it meant trying was bad. That it meant *you* were bad.

Your failures by themselves aren't so terrible, for the most part. It's how you think about them that gives them the power to shut you down.

When you fail, you experience two types of consequences: internal and external. The external consequences are what happen in the world as a result of your failure. The internal consequences are what happen inside you: the emotional impact of your failure. That math exam you botched your sophomore year? The external consequences were a bad grade and maybe a stern lecture from your parents. The internal consequences were those persistent little demons that whispered, "You're no good at math. You're too stupid to do this."

The bad grade came and went; the little voices stayed.

It's not the external result of your failure that makes it a negative experience. It's how you think about it. The external consequences of a single failure are usually small—often even insignificant. But depending on how you think about them, you can make the internal consequences colossal, even life-threatening. You've heard how many suicides there are on college campuses around exam time. And plenty of towns have an infamous "lovers' leap," where scorned romantics go to end it all, convinced that the loss of one love means they'll never love again. A single failure that by itself means hardly anything can seem as though it means *everything*.

Failures: They're a Lot Bigger on the Inside

External Consequences	Internal Consequences
Got stood up on a date	Members of the opposite sex don't like me
Lost the karate tournament	I'll never be any good at martial arts
Bounced a check	I can't handle money
Cheated on a diet	I have no willpower
Lost a client	I'm hopeless when it comes to business
Failed the exam	I'm too stupid to make it through college

Because our society views failure in a negative way, we learn to avoid trying new things. Instead of risking failure, we fall back into the comfort zone of the familiar, the tried and true. In order to avoid humiliation, we let fabulous opportunities pass us by.

But if you're going to harness the power that lies within your failures, you'll have to change the way you think about them. Learn to see them for the gifts they are.

If You Knew *This* About Failure, It Would Never Sap Your Energy Again

You have the ability to transform failures from energy siphons into energy sources. How do you do this? By recognizing that failure leads to success. It's step one in the process.

Failure is not just one possible path, it's practically the *only* path to success. It's necessary. It's required.

You can't succeed without learning. And in order to learn, you have to risk failure.

Learning doesn't happen in an atmosphere of fear. Why not? Because fear shuts down the experimentation process. People don't take risks when they're afraid. They won't try something new. And what is learning if not trying new things?

> You can't succeed if you can't grow.
> You can't grow if you can't learn.
> You can't learn if you can't fail.

Of course, there's a huge difference between appropriate and inappropriate risk. Not all risks are of equal value; not all risks are worth taking. Deciding the value of a risk is a skill like any other. Weigh the rewards of each risk against its potential outcomes, and look at the circumstances in terms of its impact on your inner vision.

Remember that not all the risks you take will pay off. You'll experience a few failures. But Quantum Success is not about one failure and then instant success. It's about failing *as many times as you need to in order to get to success.*

Why Treat Failure as a Learning Process?

In my company, we've built an extraordinary culture of learning. In our office and at our on-site trainings, we instill a thirst for learning and feedback. We use no preamble. When we give feedback on a presentation we don't start with "Last time you did it well and this time you said 'so' too often." We just say, "You said 'so' too many times." We call things done well "gems" and things that need work "opps," short for "opportunities for improvement."

After every practice presentation the group gives the person presenting three gems and three opps. We ask which they want first. When I visit camps in the summer, the facilitators ask me for opportunities. I recently visited our camp session at Wake Forest. I was particularly moved by the impact of a session. I thought it was masterful. As students left the main room and only the four facilitators were left, I went up to them to tell them how impressed I was by the session. They smiled at me in silence, then one of them said, "We're really more opportunities people. What feedback do you have for us on where we can improve?" I truly believe our staff gets the results they do and achieve the skills they have because we develop our thirst for feedback.

For many people, giving feedback takes courage. When someone takes that risk and steps forward to offer feedback, it's a treasure—and the sign of a good relationship.

You have to risk failure in order to learn anything. Whether you fail or not, risk taking alone is a powerful learning tool. But the actual experience of failing is the fastest way to learn. Failure vastly improves your odds of Quantum Success, particularly in the long run, because it tells you what to do—and what not to do—next.

When you diagnose your failures and figure out where you went wrong, you're teaching yourself, literally by trial and error, how to go right.

In my own life, my worst failures cleared the way to my greatest successes. When I lost all my money chasing dollars for the Burklyn Business School, I learned to steer clear of anything that wasn't in line with my values. It was re-applying myself to what I wanted most that led me to create SuperCamp.

> Theodore Geisel, known to generations of children as Dr. Seuss, almost gave up after his first book had been rejected by thirty publishers. He was on his way home to burn his manuscript when he happened upon an old friend who convinced him to give it one more shot. His name was Bennett Cerf. This time the publisher accepted his book.

Mistakes have special gifts to offer you. So do multiple failures. Trying over and over to achieve a particular goal is like weight lifting for the soul. Scores of bestselling authors have tales to tell about the fifty or a hundred or three hundred publishers they submitted their novels to, only to be told that they'd be better off selling insurance. But with each rejection letter, they kept submitting. They learned how to keep faith in themselves, how to keep their dreams burning bright, even under mountains of rejection letters. Their victory tasted far sweeter after a hundred rejections than it would have after only ten.

Failing is a great way to learn and grow.

Mobilize Your Failures: Turn Defeat into Victory

Congratulations—You Failed

Treat your failures as gifts. In earlier chapters, I talked about the importance of celebrating and rewarding your successes. If you're failing, it means you're giving yourself the chance to learn. You deserve credit for that.

Whenever you fail, the universe has just handed you a piece of wisdom. Don't let it go to waste. Mine it for all it's worth. Ask yourself:

- What happened?
- What did I learn?
- What will I do differently next time?

Search Your Failures for Second Chances

SuperCamp alumnus Ryan Day discovered in high school that failures themselves often contain the seeds of second chances. "As a high school senior I applied to Stonehill College. My grades were not great and my SAT scores were awful. But I thought those things weren't important and I would get in anyway. I remember my parents and brothers telling me to study hard for the SAT. I thought I knew better and didn't listen to what was great advice . . . I arrived home from school one day to a letter from Stonehill College: 'We regret to inform you that you will not be admitted to Stonehill College this semester . . .'

"I was devastated. How could this happen to me? I realized then that I hadn't worked very hard at all, and now had to face the consequences of my actions. But as I reread the letter, I found a solution to my dilemma: they suggested I apply again as a transfer student after my first semester at a different college.

This letter was not the end. They were giving me the opportunity to improve my scores and try again.

"After my first semester at St. Bonaventure University, I applied again to Stonehill and was accepted. Four years later I graduated, having turned my failure into success."

The most beautiful thing about your failures is that they're yours. No two people fail in quite the same way. Your failures are your own personal laboratory of life. In that lab you can run whatever experiments you choose. The discoveries are yours to make, the wisdom yours to keep.

"Life is a series of outcomes," says Simone Carruthers, psychologist and business consultant. "Sometimes the outcome is what you want. Great. Figure out what you did right. Sometimes the outcome is what you don't want. Great. Figure out what you did so you don't do it again."

The only time you've really failed is when you fail to learn from your mistakes.

Failure Is a Launch Pad to Quantum Success

- You up the odds of Quantum Success by learning from every failure.
- You control the internal consequences of failure by changing the way you think.

CHAPTER 10

Key Catalyst: Speak with Good Purpose

Develop the skill of speaking in a positive sense
with good intent, being responsible for honest
and direct communication.

What You'll Discover in This Chapter:

- Why it's better to be honest than to be "nice"
- How to heal damaged relationships
- How to Open The Front Door to positive communication

No one would talk much in society if they knew
how often they misunderstood others.
—*Goethe*

What's the single greatest instrument in achieving your success?

Your mouth.

What you have to say determines how far you will succeed. How so? Because Quantum Success is built on relationships, relationships are built on communication, and communication happens mostly through the spoken word.

This Key Catalyst guides you to speak positively, or as the Native American orator Rolling Thunder put it, to "speak with good purpose" (Doug Boyd, *Rolling Thunder*). Speaking with good purpose means communicating directly, clearly, honestly, and with good intent. It requires you to choose your words carefully and to take responsibility for them.

When you speak with good intent, you've already chosen the purpose of your speech before you open your mouth. You're assured that what you have to say will be beneficial to yourself and others because you've chosen your words specifically to serve this goal.

Speaking clearly and directly means that you state simply what you mean; you don't speak around the subject, hide it in metaphors, or water down its strength. You don't say you're "just a little bit angry" if, in fact, you're furious.

Speaking honestly—without the masks of sarcasm, condescension, or disdain—requires you to state your true thoughts and feelings, even if they're not pretty, even when they're not what the other person wants to hear. Honest speech is about revealing the true you.

Speaking with good purpose can be a challenge; it takes courage, effort, and practice. But until you master this skill, the quality of your relationships will be out of your hands; the satisfaction of deep, meaningful connections to others will elude you.

Why Speak with Good Purpose?

Words are powerful. They can build or destroy.

A few cutting words, let loose in a moment of anger, can wound someone for a lifetime. Remember when your best friend in high school said you had a "lame smile," when your uncle quipped about your "bird legs," or your teacher discouraged you from going after that high-octane math class because "you're no good at numbers"? I remember to this day the pain I felt hearing my mother snickering to her friend in the stands at the ice skating rink, watching me flounder. Hurtful comments can stay with you a long time.

On the other hand, you've had times when a few kind words made all the difference. Have you ever had someone whisper, "I believe you can do it," just when you needed to hear it the most?

Communication is the bridge between people—it's the glue that holds all relationships together. It's what forms the link between husband and wife, between parent and child, between teacher and student, between friends, siblings, partners, and co-workers.

Your relationships thrive or wither depending on the quality of the communication that serves them.

> Success is built on relationships; relationships are built
> on communication.

Patterns of speaking become the accepted ways to interact. Look how many marriages fall into ruin when husband and wife slip into nagging, accusations, and blame. Think of the friendships that have disintegrated because of a misunderstanding that was never cleared up. Consider budding relationships that never went any further because one party or the other wasn't willing to take the communication to a deeper level.

In any relationship, positive communication creates a healthy environment, just as random, ill-intentioned communication creates a toxic one. When relationships aren't strong, apathy and distrust have room to grow. How productive can anyone be in an environment like that?

On the other end of the spectrum, when relationships come first, when the atmosphere is one of joy, trust, and safety, people function at a higher level. They're more loyal, and they're prepared to do whatever it takes to get the job done. Our SuperCamp staffers sometimes stay until midnight painting posters, organizing paperwork—doing whatever needs to be done. They don't put in these hours because they have to; they do it because they love what they're doing and it means so much to them to get it done right. You'd never see this kind of dedication in a workplace dominated by fear.

The same dynamics make or break families. A colleague once told me how she'd visited the house of a college friend and discovered a TV blaring in almost every room—even in the bathroom. The friend's mother, father, and sisters seemed to be using the noise from the TVs as barricades to keep from interacting with one another. The tension in that household was palpable. Communication was nonexistent.

But, the same colleague recalled, the environment was completely different at another friend's house. Dad, daughter, mom, and son went about their day in a spirit of affectionate laughter and silliness. Since the mom was from Denmark, they kept the Danish tradition of hosting a coming-of-age party for their daughter, my colleague's friend. She remembers how bright her friend's eyes were when she stood in the center of a circle of loving family who took turns reciting made-up poems and singing goofy little songs that told the highlights of her life. The communication in that family was loving, supportive, and joyful. Who wouldn't want to grow up in a family like that?

Words matter. I don't know who came up with that phrase about "sticks and stones," but they were wrong. Words can hurt. They can also heal. What you say has an impact.

How to Speak and Listen Positively

How do you make it happen? How do you direct your speech to forge strong bonds and create safe environments? How can you make sure you're speaking with good purpose?

Speaking with good purpose begins with taking control of your thoughts. We tend to assume our thoughts are beyond our control, that they come to us unbidden. But we can train our thoughts just like we train our willpower. My partner at Burklyn Business School, Marshall Thurber, used to introduce this Key Catalyst with a reading from Doug Boyd's *Rolling Thunder*:

> People have to be responsible for their thoughts, so they have to learn to control them. It's not easy, but it can be done. First of all, if we don't want to think certain things, we don't say them. We don't have to eat everything we see, and we don't have to say everything we think. So we begin by watching our words and speaking with good purpose only. There are times when we need clean and pure minds with no unwanted thoughts and we have to train and prepare steadily for those times until we are ready . . . there is no use condemning yourself. You don't have to pay attention to those unwanted thoughts. If they keep coming into your head, just leave them alone and say, "I don't choose to have such thoughts" and they will

soon go away ... keep a steady determination and stick with that purpose ...

Listen carefully to what that little voice is trying to get you to believe about other people. Because if you don't recognize what the voice is saying, its negative influence may be creeping into your speech. Ask yourself, "Am I saying something useful right now? Are my words encouraging or damaging?"

You don't have to say everything you think.

Speaking with good purpose makes a difference at all times, but it becomes vital when people aren't getting along. It's hard to communicate negative feelings without slipping into negative patterns: laying blame, attacking, accusing, insulting. But to get at the heart of this Key Catalyst, recognize that these behaviors don't accomplish anything positive. The only power they have is to damage, confuse, wound feelings, and inspire the other person to respond in kind. But bring in positive speech, and even in a tense atmosphere, you'll have a chance to forge a bond of communication. Positive speech opens a path for discussing disagreements, clearing up miscommunication, and creating solutions.

The goal of positive speaking and active listening is to keep communication flowing. It's as much about hearing the other person as it is about making yourself heard. When someone is speaking, don't use the time to formulate your own opinion or response. Instead, focus all your efforts on understanding what the person is telling you. When the person is finished speaking, rephrase what he's said and ask if you're correct.

Catch Yourself—Why Was I Going to Say That?

Positive communication is a habit. It's a matter of training yourself to monitor your thoughts before they become speech.

With practice, you'll learn to focus on giving words to positive thoughts, to recognizing people's strengths, and to offering praise and encouragement.

Don't *avoid* expressing negative thoughts, feelings, and experiences, but learn to recognize them for what they are before you say them. Treat a negative thought like a wasp that gets into the house. Don't overreact; don't throw lots of energy at it. Simply think, "Okay, what am I going to do about that?"

If it's simply a random unpleasant thought, you don't like that person's whiny tone or wish another person wasn't so pushy, acknowledge the thought and let it go. Choose not to give it the power of spoken words. But if it's one that needs resolution, you may need to express it.

Handle these times carefully. Think about the intention of your words. Are they meant to support the person and build a stronger relationship? Are they focused on finding a solution? Speaking positively is not just about what to communicate but what to *avoid* communicating. Gossip, complaints, and nagging are destructive ways of airing negative thoughts. They pollute the atmosphere in which your relationships are growing. Instead, let the pressure out of these negative thoughts by saying them in a supportive context. Give them words in the context of healing and preserving the relationship. Listen to the difference between, "You're sloppy; you live like a pig," and "I'm uncomfortable sharing a room with you because we have different ideas about tidiness." The same idea, expressed without barbs, is a far more accurate statement of the situation.

Don't Muck the Conversation

Beware—some speech that seems beneficial on the surface can impede positive communication.

How often have you heard these well-intentioned phrases?

"You don't need to lose weight; you look fine."

"Now, if I were you . . ."

"I know exactly what you mean. The same thing happened to me . . ."

People usually mean well when they say these things, but they actually impede productive communication because they deny other people's feelings. Reassurance, advice, and identification actually shut down the flow of communication. I call this "mucking the conversation."

You know what muck is. You've stepped in it. It's a mix of mud, goo, and maybe a little manure that sticks to your feet and makes it harder for you to get anywhere. That's exactly what you introduce into a conversation when you throw in these well-meaning phrases.

When people share a feeling, an experience, or a fear, and you respond with reassurance, you may mean to comfort them, but what you're really doing is cutting off their sharing with the statement that they shouldn't feel that way: "Don't feel what you're feeling. You have no reason to feel that way." End of conversation.

When they communicate a problem they're having, and you hand them a solution, you shut them down. Think of it this way: how could you find a solution to their problem in five minutes, when for weeks, months, or years, they haven't found one? They're the ones *living it*. You've just placed yourself in a position of superiority to them—a position you haven't earned. They're not likely to share their problems with you in the future.

When a person begins to tell you about something that he's going through, and you cut him off with, "I know exactly how you feel . . . me too," you've killed the communication. The speaker never gets to finish. You never get to find out whether his experience was anything like yours. Besides, even if your experiences are similar, they'll never be exactly the same.

Don't muck the conversation with reassurance, advice, or identification. Your goal is not to diagnose, pacify, or fix. Let your goal be to listen, and to let the speaker know he's been heard.

Which Is Kinder—Being Honest or Being "Nice"?

As a child, you learned: "If you can't say something nice, don't say anything at all." You wanted to be liked—we all do—so you tried to make yourself likable. When you thought something less-than-flattering about people, you learned to tell them the opposite of what you really thought.

But was that really kind?

Suppose your friend comes to you needing an honest opinion: "Does this hair color look good on me?"

Let's say you really think it makes her look awful. But you don't want to hurt her feelings, so you tell her, "You look fine."

How good of a friend are you being?

Tell her a "little white lie," and you might spare her some uncomfortable feelings—temporarily. But tell her the truth, and you could help her improve her appearance. You do need to be kind. You do need to be supportive. But be honest.

Telling her what you think, and the degree to which you think it, is a risk. It could lose you the friendship entirely. But it's also the only way to deepen your relationship because it's the only way to be a true friend. If she can't take the honesty, and goes away, she was not that good a friend in the first place. As a true friend, you're devoted to your friend's growth, which means you have to be willing to talk about the places where she needs to grow. Turn it the other way around: To be a true friend means you can accept criticism from your friend without anger.

At SuperCamp we teach that NICE stands for Nothing Inside Cares Enough—to tell the truth, to support the person's growth.

Being honest and direct is kinder than being NICE.

Let People Know What You're Thinking

"Got a minute?"

Have you ever had someone ask you this? Doesn't it immediately send up a yellow flag in your mind: *Why is he asking me this? Does he want me to have a cup of coffee with him or does he want a favor?*

It's an evasive question. It'll probably be met with an evasive answer: "Why are you asking?"

"I want to know if you're free to do something."

"Well, I'll have to check my schedule . . ."

And on the dance goes. Your truthful answer is probably, *It depends on what that "something" is.* But you don't feel comfortable coming out with it so bluntly. You feel as though you're being cornered.

I get this a lot at work—and I catch myself doing it sometimes. I handle it by reminding the person to be visible: "Why are you asking?" or "Tell me more."

It's much better to say, "do you have a minute . . ." and complete the sentence with, " . . . to _____."

When your goal is to speak with good purpose, make your communication visible. Visible communication makes your purpose clear; invisible communication, as in the example above, masks your purpose.

When your intent is clear, people don't feel as if they're being tricked or manipulated. They feel safe and respected. And they'll feel comfortable responding to you in kind. They'll give your direct communication a direct answer.

Visible communication, a vital component of speaking with good purpose, grows stronger relationships. It's about making your intent "visible," making your wishes known.

OTFD: Open the Front Door

In my company we teach two powerful tools for achieving clear, constructive communication. The first is an acronym to help you get a communication across; the second is a method for apologizing when you've wronged someone. Notice that both these tools are focused on letting go of negatives and moving forward with positives.

In our programs we teach people to Open the Front Door when they want to communicate something. It's particularly good for communicating something you're upset about, but it can be used in almost any scenario, with almost anyone.

OTFD communicates four vital pieces of information: Observation, Thought, Feeling, and Desire:

Observation: "I noticed that twice this month, you made plans with me in advance, then at the last minute you canceled them to do something else."

Thought: "I thought when you did that it meant time with me wasn't very important to you, or that your plans with me were only until something more interesting to do came along."

Feeling: "Each time you canceled your plans with me, I felt frustrated and neglected. I felt lonely."

Desire: "In the future, I'd like you to only make plans with me that you intend to keep. If you think something more interesting is likely to come up, please don't schedule anything with me."

Following these four steps tells the other person precisely what they need to know in order to understand you. Often, you'll find when you finish communicating this way, the person you're talking to will agree: "Yes, I see why you feel this way." Compare this to what happens when you try to express an upset through blame, shame, judgment, or ridicule, and you'll see the power in this tool.

Apologize with These Four Steps and Heal the Damage

OTFD's twin sister is the four-part apology. Take these four steps when you're on the other end of the communication, when you've wronged or hurt someone, or when you've made a mistake significant enough to impact someone else:

1. Acknowledge: Take responsibility for what you've done. Use "I statements" to show that you're the one behind the action: "I acknowledge that I canceled our time at the last minute more than once and that this is upsetting."

2. Apologize: "I apologize for hurting you by wasting your time and making you feel unwanted."

3. Make It Right: Ask, "How can I make it right?" If the other person doesn't have something specific in mind, offer something to make up for the thing you failed to give before. "Since you lost what could have been a wonderful Saturday, is there something you'd like to do together next Saturday that would make up for it?"

4. Recommit: Show that you're following a plan to keep the upset from happening in the future. "From now on, if I make plans with you, unless a real emergency comes up, I'll keep them."

> I believe the words "I apologize" are much more powerful than "sorry." How often have you heard a nonchalant "I'm sorry," as if that would change anything?
>
> At one of the schools where our methods are used, the principal caught a young grade-schooler doing something that was against the rules. The girl mumbled a defiant "Sorry."
>
> The principal said, "You know, Elizabeth, in this school we use a four-part apology."
>
> The little girl replied, "Sorry, sorry, sorry, sorry."
>
> I guess she didn't quite learn the process! But it did get a laugh from the principal.

The four-part apology's power lies in its ability to demonstrate that you're taking responsibility for your actions. When the people in your life realize you're willing and able to do that, they'll be more open and trusting with you. Your relationships will be better.

Clearing the air of arguments releases tensions and feels fabulous. It releases positive energy and creates synergy, especially if it's an argument that's been festering for a long time. In the light of clear, positive communication, even long-standing miscommunications can be resolved. People whose relationships have faltered for years can get back on track when they apologize with this level of responsibility.

Speaking with good purpose allows you to harness the awesome power of words. When you speak positively, honestly, and directly, with the goal of keeping relationships strong, words cease to be a random force and begin to direct their awesome energy in the service of your dream.

Montessori's Peace Rose Cleanses Relationships of Hurt Feelings

In many Montessori classrooms, you'll find a small plastic rose sitting in a bud vase. This is the Peace Rose; its purpose is to help kids learn to resolve disputes.

Whenever kids argue, or a disagreement arises between teacher and student, the arguing parties sit down holding the Peace Rose between them. They tell how they felt about the incident in question and discuss how each party is going to change behavior in the future. When the discussion is concluded, the people holding the rose say, "I declare peace." And with that, the dispute ends.

The Peace Rose helps kids practice the skill of conflict resolution. But most importantly, it teaches them to *let go of an argument.* Left to fester, bad feelings act like a cancer in a relationship. This quietly powerful ritual provides a means to finish a dispute so that the relationship is cleared of its harmful aftereffects.

You can adapt Montessori's Peace Rose and make it your own: Turn it into a Peace Feather, Peace Telephone, Peace Statue—whatever symbol says resolution to you.

Speaking with Good Purpose Gives You the Power

- Replace an environment of fear with one of trust.
- Speak your mind honestly and constructively when you have negative feedback that will serve others.
- Repair damaged relationships by apologizing with the Four-Part Apology.
- Build stronger, deeper relationships.

CHAPTER 11

Key Catalyst: This Is It!

Each moment, each task counts. Develop the ability
to focus your attention on the present moment.
How much attention you pay to *now* determines the
quality of your tomorrow.

What You'll Discover in This Chapter:

- Secret wisdom is revealed to you when you focus on the now
- What to say back to that little voice that tries to distract you from the moment
- How to turn boring tasks into magic moments

Unease, anxiety, tension, stress, worry—all forms of fear—
are caused by too much future and not enough present.
—*Eckhart Tolle,* The Power of Now

A friend of mine told me she used to have trouble living in the now. She was always focused on what was coming five or ten years down the road. When she was in college, she couldn't wait to graduate and tackle the "real world." When she was starting her career, she couldn't stop obsessing about getting married and starting her family. Then when the kids came, she was forever daydreaming about life after wiping runny noses and sitting through Little League games. Her kids couldn't grow up quick enough to suit her.

Then one day she was standing in line at the grocery store going over future plans in her mind, nearly oblivious to her two grade-schoolers bantering cutely beside her. She half-noticed an elderly woman standing in line behind them, smiling at the children's antics. Just as the friend was finishing her check-out, the elderly woman tugged at her sleeve and, with a twinkle in her eye, whispered, "You know this is the best time of your life, don't you?"

My friend felt a tingle. She knew she'd been told something. She thought, "My kids are with me *now*; they won't always be. If I wish away these next ten years, I'll never get this time back."

Are you like my friend, waiting for the next moment while the present one slips away?

We all struggle with this tendency. We get bored, distracted, anxious. We fall victim to the "grass is greener" syndrome, thinking what's coming has to be better than what's here. We're always looking ahead for something more exciting. But when we do this, we pay a price. We miss out on the only part of our lives where we can actually make a difference—the only part of lives where we actually *live*: now.

For another thing, it's more fun to live in the now. Think of it this way: how much do you like waiting? If you're forever waiting for the future to arrive, you're waiting—forever. There's no value in frittering away the present over the future because the future never arrives. The only moment that counts is the one that's already in your hands. This is it!

When you're fully engaged in the now, life is more exciting and fulfilling. You'll enjoy what you're doing more, get more out of it, and be better at it.

For another thing, focusing on the present changes your perspective. When you put all your energy into the current task, you are living with the maximum vibrancy. You begin to see each task differently. You will focus, maximizing your intensity. You'll see solutions you didn't recognize before. You'll come up with short-cuts for routine tasks. And you'll develop greater insight and intuition about what you're doing.

When you live fully in the present, you take full advantage of the gifts that are coming your way. You learn the lessons the current task has to offer. You seize the moment. You gather your rose-buds while you may, and you also take the opportunity to hand out a few. Living in the now doesn't just make you more effective; it's the *only way* to be effective, because it's the only chance you have to make an impact. Imagine a champion tennis player, like Venus Williams or Roger Federer, *not* living in the now. You can't do anything about the past, and the only thing you can do about the future is make tentative plans. But, as all champion athletes know, when you live in the now, you have the power.

It's an awesome tool.

The Value of Time

To realize the value of *one year*, ask the student who failed a grade.

To realize the value of *one month*, ask a mother who gave birth to a premature baby.

To realize the value of *one week*, ask the editor of a weekly newspaper.

To realize the value of *one hour*, ask the lovers who are waiting to meet.

To realize the value of *one minute*, ask a person who missed the bus.

To realize the value of *one second*, ask the person who just avoided an accident.

To realize the value of *one millisecond*, ask the person who won a silver medal in the Olympics.

—Anonymous

We once had an inspiring SuperCamp participant named John who made a tremendous impact on the staff as well as on his fellow campers. He walked on crutches, but rather than let that slow him down or dampen his spirits, he was one of the most enthusiastic participants—in every activity—that we've ever had. He even lifted the spirits of another camper with a serious physical disability. Whenever the other camper started feeling sorry for himself, John would bring him back to the pure joy of the present and the power of keeping a "This is it" attitude no matter what life has dealt you. He was the living embodiment of throwing himself joyfully into the moment.

When people live in the now, it affects everyone around them.

There's another compelling reason to live in the present: It's the single greatest determiner of the quality of your tomorrows. If you spend this moment focused on tomorrow, you sabotage the quality of those tomorrows. Only by focusing on what you're doing now can you affect what your life will be like in the future. Waste the present fretting about the future, then when the future becomes the now, it will come with little reward.

Each Task Counts; Each Event Teaches

When you live each moment knowing that this is it, you'll be able to see what people who are frittering away the present don't see: every moment has a gift.

You'll discover that every moment has something to teach you—if you're looking for the lesson. Even if it's a task you've done a thousand times, there's something new to see in it, or a new way to look at it, if you're prepared to look.

You'll find that every moment presents a chance that may never come again, whether it's an opportunity to commend, apologize, make a friend, say thank you, or make a difference. These little magical opportunities can come and go in a twinkling. You'll miss most of them if you're not on the lookout.

And sometimes, when you take your focus off the future and put it back onto the present, you'll find that the things you were daydreaming about are not in some far-off other time, but right under your nose.

> The work I do often requires me to jump into the moment. Once when a charter school system had finalized all the details for Quantum Learning in their schools, I attended a meeting to celebrate the event and to tell the excited crowd more about our programs. I was on my way up to the stage when someone

pulled me aside and told me funding for Quantum Learning had been cut from the grant at the last moment. Instead of the enthusiastic speech I had planned, I had to improvise a speech of an entirely different nature.

Another time I went on a speaking tour in China that took me far from my comfort zone. Rather than knowing the topic and preparing well in advance, I would arrive at each new stop with no idea what I would be expected to say. I'd sometimes discover the topic on the way to the podium. By the end of that tour, I'd learned a lot about thinking on my feet!

How to Make This Moment It—*Especially* if It's Not What You Expected

How do you become distracted from the moment? Often we get ambushed by that nagging little voice that whispers to us about chores to be done, unfinished projects, worries, regrets, inadequacies, and a never-ending swarm of "what-ifs," most of which never come to pass. That voice is always trying to steal your attention away from the task at hand.

That insidious voice in your head not only devours your focus, it can also eat away at your self-confidence. It whispers defeatist messages: "You don't know how to do that. You're not smart enough. People will think you're crazy. What will your mother think?"

It's difficult to resist that little voice. If it tells us we're going to fail, often as not, we will fail.

How do you end the tyranny of the little voice? You take control of it. You turn it to your advantage. First, make yourself aware of what it's telling you. Move that voice to the forefront of your consciousness and expose its messages. Whenever you hear that voice make a negative comment, counter it with a positive one. When it tries to tell you that you can't, say, "Yes, I can."

Sometimes you don't focus on the moment simply because you don't enjoy the task at hand. It's not the voice's fault at times like these. Sometimes you just get bored, tired, or lonely. Then what?

You could easily make the mistake of focusing on something else when you're doing a task you don't like—a kind of mental chewing gum to distract you from the unpleasantness of the moment. But doing this is a mistake, because then you miss the gift that moment has to offer you.

Instead of avoiding the task, reframe it. Change the way you look at it. When you don't like a task, discover the value in it. If you can't uncover enough value in the task itself, then find it in the character you're building by performing it.

If you want to find the true importance in any given task, call up the big picture. Weigh what you're doing now against your vision and see where it fits in. Make it a habit.

Living in the now gets easier with practice. Try using a device to remind yourself: a watch or a ring, a sticker on your phone, or an object with "This is it!" written on it. Whenever you find you're drifting away from the moment, pull yourself back into the now.

> When you recognize that this moment is it, you're open to the gifts it has to offer. Some of the best memories I have are all about being fully present in simple moments. Eating lemon meringue pie with my dad and talking about how airplanes fly. Asking him how refrigerators worked. Eating cooked blueberries in the kitchen late at night. Telling stories with my grandkids in their hideout under the basement stairs. Watching tiger lily blossoms open with my husband Joe. Little moments contain great magic.

This Is It!

- Living in the moment is more fun than living in some imagined future.
- When that little voice tries to distract you, talk back. Tell it you're up to the challenge.
- Reframe: transform boring tasks into moments of inspiration by focusing on the big picture.
- Focus on the now, and you'll seize opportunities to learn, love, connect, and transform.
- When your worries are so strong that you can't focus on the now, stop what you're doing and analyze your options. Make an action plan. Then go back to the now.

CHAPTER 12

Key Catalyst: Commit Yourself

Make a commitment: follow your vision without
wavering; stay the course. Do whatever it takes.

What You'll Discover in This Chapter:

- The real reason why committed people seem so fortunate
- Why commitment has the power to change the world

Whatever you can do, or dream you can, begin it.
Boldness has genius, power, and magic in it.
—*Goethe*

One of our facilitators tells a terrific audience-participation story to illustrate the difference commitment makes. "Let's say you decide to be a high-dive champion," he tells his audience. "You run right out and you buy a body suit tailor-made for high diving and all the equipment and accessories. Is that commitment?"

The group shouts back, "No!"

"Next, you enroll in high-diving classes and you learn all about high diving. Are you committed now?"

"No!" the group shouts.

"Okay, you enroll in your first competition. You climb the ladder and step out onto the board. Committed now?"

"No!"

"You dive off the board. You're in mid-air. *Now* are you committed?"

The audience shouts, "YES!"

Commitment is all about that moment when there's no turning back—the magic that results when you're truly committed. It's a mind-set: there are no other options. There are no more debates, no mind games, no procrastination. There is only action, single-minded, focused, and pure. That commitment wields a mighty power and brings with it an intense joy.

We call it WIT: Doing Whatever It Takes.

During a vision day, I did an activity called "Who's on the Bus?" The bus symbolized the commitment our staffers had made to the company's vision. I had a pop-up bus that several people could get in as a prop. I also set up chairs in rows to look like bus seats.

One by one, staff members came up to me, looked me in the eyes, made a commitment to be on the bus, and took a seat. Later that year, a staff member told me that a company had been trying to hire her away from us, offering her more money and benefits. She told me that whenever she was tempted, what went through her mind was that she had made a commitment to be on the bus. She understood clearly that being with us fulfilled her purpose, where the other position was simply a job for money.

When you realize that every dream worth pursuing involves challenges, you discover that commitment is an absolute necessity. It's what makes the difference between giving up and going on.

Commitment alone has the power to change the world.

Midnight, Lake Michigan, 1927

One dark winter night, a man stood on the shore of Lake Michigan, preparing to swim out into the icy waters and drown. This man considered himself a total failure: He'd been expelled from Harvard twice. He'd lost more jobs than he could count, and had lost his infant daughter to a horrible disease. He was in so much pain that he actually took comfort in the prospect of sinking through the icy waters into oblivion. Before he stepped into the lake, he paused to review his life. He discovered, to his surprise, that it was rich with experiences and knowledge. A thought struck him: what if he used his storehouse of information to help people? What could he lose? If it didn't work, the lake would always be here.

He decided to see what would happen if he looked at his life differently; he called it an experiment in "making the world work." He committed himself to examining every aspect of his life and pledging it to the service of humankind. His experiment resulted in some of the greatest achievements of the twentieth century.

Within his lifetime, Buckminster Fuller held twenty-seven patents, received forty-seven honorary degrees, wrote more than twenty books, was heralded as a poet, educator, engineer, mathematician, artist, and more. He was called the Leonardo DaVinci of our time. And it was all due to the commitment he made back in 1927 on the icy midnight shore of Lake Michigan.

Why Commitment?

Let me sketch for you what your quest looks like without commitment. Then let's look at the difference commitment makes.

Let's say you're going after something extremely difficult. You don't need commitment to achieve the easy. You want to publish your novel? Join the ranks of thousands of new would-be novelists who try and fail each year. You plan to make the Olympic swim team next year? You're seeking entry into a group so elite that only a handful of excellent swimmers ever make it. You want to become CEO of a wildly successful company? Join the melee of highly qualified candidates, some of whom will stop at nothing to one-up you. Whatever your dream, let's assume it's something extremely challenging—and extremely worthwhile.

Let's say you get up enough courage to go for it, but you haven't really made a commitment. You tell yourself, "Well, I'll try." You're not committed to doing whatever it takes to succeed. In fact, you've given yourself an out. Now, when you fall short of the mark, you can say, "Well, I tried."

Trying doesn't work. When you're not committed, you leave a crack open for hesitation. Hesitation leaks energy. Energy leaks reduce the chance of Quantum Success.

Without commitment, you stay focused on what is rather than what could be. You don't see how to achieve the impossible because it still looks impossible. You don't see the tiny path up the mountainside that will get you over the top because you're too busy staring at the mountain in its enormity.

Now let's look at the same scenario when you're committed.

Commitment allows you to switch your focus to what's possible. You become like Alice going through the looking glass. One minute, you're looking at yourself, just as you are; the next, you're looking at a whole new world that you couldn't see a moment before. And all because you took a single step forward. That one step was all it took to punch through from the limited "what is" to the unlimited "what can be." The force that propelled the step: commitment.

Let's say you win the job of your dreams, but after two days at work you realize the workload is far beyond your skill. Without commitment, all you see is yourself in your present form: inadequate. You're certain you'll mess up, disgrace yourself, and get fired, so you quit to avoid the pain of failure.

If you went into the new job with the commitment to give it all you've got, whether you believed you could do it or not, your mind's eye would see the competent employee that you could be a month from now, with the proper training and some practice, boldly reaching and exceeding the company's expectations. That vision would become reality for you, and all your efforts would go into making it happen.

Commitment is the ultimate expression of free will. Without it, things look impossible, and you give in to appearances. With it, you're able to keep on moving forward, in spite of discouraging circumstances.

Why Power and Good Fortune Follow Commitment

A friend told me of a beloved piano teacher from childhood who used to fly into a passion when anybody would say, "Gee, it must be nice to be so talented, to have the gift of playing so well." These people, the pianist complained, seemed to think her musical ability just descended on her like a magic spell: One minute she was all thumbs; the next, she was breezily pouring Prokofiev onto the keys. They didn't see the long hours of boring scales, the Saturday outings traded away for more practice time, the fingers so sore that they had to be soaked in warm water. All they saw were the results, which looked effortless. I do believe that there's such a thing as natural talent, but the world is full of talented people who don't accomplish much. It takes commitment to develop what's there.

To the uncommitted, the committed look strangely fortunate. Happy circumstances just seem to land in their laps. They seem, almost uncannily, to meet the people they need to know and find the opportunities they need to find. They see solutions where others only see obstacles. But the committed will tell you it's not because they view things differently than the non-committed; it's because they never stop looking for a way to make their dreams happen.

That's the primary characteristic of committed people: they're driven by their dreams. Odds are, you've known—and possibly been driven crazy by—people like this. But they're infinitely rewarding to know.

A quantum difference exists between finding that passion and merely giving your word. Committed people behave like people in love—commitment is much like a love affair. Haven't you known people who were indifferent to marriage until they fell head over heels in love? It's a passion. The cynical might even call it an obsession. But there are things in this world that can only be accomplished within the blast furnace of obsession.

Some things that are worth doing take an extraordinary amount of fire. I would never have been able to turn SuperCamp into a reality without a quantum passion. I held onto my intention to make it happen, throughout all the challenging times. Giving up was never an option in my mind. I held the intention so firmly that it created a mass of energy, a vision that others could see, touch, hold, and believe in.

Throw Yourself Into Your Vision

This is how you harness the power of commitment: you find out what you love passionately enough to give it all you've got, then you give it.

Commitment can spring from anything that inspires strong feeling. It can be motivated by a deeply felt desire, a strongly held principle, or the desire to make a difference in people's lives.

It comes down to a simple moment of decision: will you, or will you not, do whatever it takes?

Once you've made the vow to follow your passion no matter what, your commitment carries you through. It's the "no matter what" part that holds all the power. You're locked into staying the course. You may feel discouraged, even hopeless. You may lose all your confidence in yourself. It doesn't matter. None of it matters. You've vowed to go on trying *no matter what*. Circumstances become irrelevant in the face of commitment.

No matter what inspires you, no matter how you approach it, in order to harness the titanic strength of commitment, let your passion take over. Give yourself permission to lose yourself utterly in what you love. You'll have no choice but to commit.

Commitment Has the Power to Change the World

- Commitment is the desire to do *whatever it takes* to make your vision happen.
- Commitment carries you through when all your other reserves have failed.
- Commitment calls forth help from unexpected sources.

CHAPTER 13

Key Catalyst: Take Ownership

Be someone who can be counted upon,
someone who responds.

What You'll Discover in This Chapter:

- The power and pleasure that comes from being in control of yourself
- The secret to overcoming mistakes and healing damaged relationships
- How to win the ownership game

To be a man is to be responsible. It is to feel shame at the sight of what
seems to be unmerited misery. It is to take pride in a victory won
by one's comrades. It is to feel, when setting one's stone, that one is
contributing to the building of the world.
—Antoine De Saint-Exupery

Remember your first car? You were so proud of it. You polished it, vacuumed it, bought accessories to dress it up. Okay, so it was a twenty-year-old clunker with rust holes in the fenders. But it was yours! Just claiming that car as your own made you feel proud.

When you claim ownership of your actions and your attitude, you feel fantastic about yourself. When you own your behavior, you'll feel the same surge of power and pride you felt over that fine piece of rolling steel you owned in your youth.

Taking ownership is all about accountability, taking ownership of what you do and think—including your mistakes, your excuses, your failures to act, and actions that you're less than proud of.

Dismantle the word "accountability," and you'll see that it literally means the ability to be counted on. It means you're willing to take responsibility for the choices you make. It means accepting responsibility for making change happen, whether personally or globally. Bottom line, it means whether things go wrong or right, you point to yourself as the cause. You're accountable.

Why Accountability?

Why hold yourself accountable? What does accountability do for you?

Accountability puts you in control. It allows you to make things happen. It makes you a potent force in your own life.

Many years ago, a high-profile person did something while at SuperCamp that had the potential to hurt our reputation. The person came to me and apologized. She looked me right in the eyes, took full ownership of her actions, and said she would do whatever I wanted to make it right. I was impressed with her sincerity and never told anyone about the incident. If she hadn't apologized so thoroughly and sincerely, I'd have thought less of her. As it was, my esteem of her was, in some ways, higher than it had been before the incident.

Accountability is a whole-life concept. You can take ownership of your career, relationship, finances, education, fitness—all areas of your life. You can create a massive shift in your life simply by taking ownership of your attitude.

Accountability not only puts you in control, it makes you feel terrific. The great feelings that come with accountability are self-reinforcing: when you enjoy a certain pride of ownership over your own life, you take better care of the things that are your responsibility. You'll give your best effort and, as a result, enjoy greater rewards.

Pride of Ownership Looks Great on You

What's pride of ownership? It's that glowing feeling you have about something that's yours. Pride of ownership inspires you to take special care of the things you possess. You've probably felt this way about clothes you've owned, maybe furniture, real estate, artwork, or pets. But you can enjoy pride of ownership in nonmaterial things too.

When you own the things you think and do, you'll experience pride of ownership, and you'll be inspired to "take special care" of your actions and your attitude. Pride of ownership shows in your posture, in your voice, in your whole bearing. When you own what you do, you walk tall, speak with confidence, and draw people to you.

When You Pass the Buck, You Abdicate Power

When you pass the buck, you volunteer for powerlessness. You make yourself a passive ingredient in the recipe of your own life. You remove yourself from the equation.

How often have you heard, or said, these refusals of ownership?

"I couldn't help it."

"I would have called, but Larry had my cell phone."

"The sun was in my eyes."

"The people in sales didn't get me the numbers on time."

"I wouldn't have said it if you hadn't made me so angry."

"I'm late because my kids didn't get ready on time."

"It's not my fault."

How good does it make you feel to fall back on lines like these? It doesn't generate pride or boost your energy. It does the opposite. Denying responsibility doesn't make the problem go away. Statements like, "I didn't know I was supposed to work on that report. I never agreed to that," cause frustration and make you look unreliable and even dishonest. It might take some of the immediate heat off you, but it does little to relieve the feelings of guilt and incompetence that come when you know you've let somebody down.

And that's the worst part of passing the buck: it erodes your relationships. It marks you as someone who can't be counted on. And, as I've said throughout this book, relationships are at the heart of success.

If you're after Quantum Success, the buck stops with you.

The Responsibility's Yours Whether You Take It or Not

Rob Dunton, Quantum Learning Network alumnus, wrote of accountability: "A few months ago, I was in Tijuana, Mexico. I passed a little boy on the street. He was curled up, fast asleep, clutching a battered guitar in one hand and a cup with a few pesos in the other. I dropped a five-dollar bill in his cup, then I walked on, happy to be an anonymous giver.

The money would be a huge help to him, whether he knew who gave it or not.

Years ago, when I was a teenager, a friend of mine and I were playing "air guitar" in the basement with my parents' guitars. Our heavy-metal moves got pretty wild, and I cracked the neck on one guitar. I thought, *It's not all that noticeable; I'll put it back and no one will know.*

But the guitar was just as broken, whether I took responsibility for it or not."

Rob realized that by refusing to own what he did, he'd turned one negative into two: The guitar was broken, and his parents would feel awful that whoever broke it—and it wouldn't take long for them to guess that it was him—would betray their relationship by shirking the responsibility. Rob realized later that if he'd owned what he did, he could have turned the negative into a positive. He could have shown his parents what a great kid they were raising by owning up to what he did and working to fix it.

Play the Ownership Game

Let's play a game. On a blank piece of paper, draw a horizontal line. Above the line, write the words *Choices, Accountability, Freedom,*

Responsibility, and *Willingness*. Below the line, write *Laying Blame*, *Justification*, *Denial*, and *Quitting*.

Here's how you play the ownership game: Pick something you did recently. Did you start off the week arguing with your spouse? Did you follow through with your plans to go to the gym for a workout after work? Did you hide that credit card bill from yourself because it was much larger than you'd expected? Did you apologize to a client for missing a deadline, and outline a plan for getting that project back on schedule? For each action you identify, examine what you did and determine whether you were playing above the line or below the line.

When you're playing above the line, you're taking responsibility, being accountable for your actions, and looking for solutions. You're taking ownership. Playing above the line wins you freedom, trust, and success. Above the line, you're not a victim of circumstances because you determine how you'll respond to them.

When you're playing below the line, you're blaming others for your mistakes, justifying your actions, denying them, or quitting before you reach your goal. Below the line, you act as if circumstances are beyond your control. It's not your fault; there's nothing you can do about it. You live in complacency and inaction. It *seems* easier than playing above the line, until you realize you're not getting anywhere.

Now comes the most important part. Instead of reflecting on past activities, play the ownership game in the present. In each moment, check yourself: "Which side of the line am I on?" The object of the game is to put yourself above the line in every action and interaction. When you find yourself slipping below the line, put yourself back on top.

Playing Above the Line

Choices   Accountability   Freedom   Responsibility   Willingess

---

Laying Blame   Justification   Denial   Quitting

Playing Below the Line

Communicate Your Ownership

One day a few years ago, I got hung up in rush-hour traffic and arrived twenty minutes late for an important meeting. The person I was meeting looked upset. I started to say, "I got stuck in traffic and couldn't help it,"—ducking the blame. Instead, I said, "I knew traffic was heavy this time of day, and I should have left earlier. I know I've cost you time waiting for me. Would you like to stay later than we planned? Next time, I'll leave earlier." Instantly, the anger melted from my associate's face. We charged ahead into our meeting in an upbeat mood.

Take Responsibility for *All* Aspects of Your Life

You may not be able to control everything that happens in your life, but you can control your *reaction* to what happens.

Last summer, irate parents came to me with a complaint. Another child had allegedly taken something from their daughter, and they had decided that somehow it was all my fault. They said I had ruined their vacation. They went on and on about it when they could have chosen to put this minor incident behind them and still enjoyed their holiday.

You're in control of your own conditioning. If you're in the habit of backpedaling and buck-passing, you can recondition your response. Remember Pavlov's dogs? Whenever Pavlov fed his dogs, he rang a bell. Soon, the dogs associated the sound of the bell with food and would salivate whenever the bell rang. If you're accustomed to responding to failures with blame, denial, and excuses, it's time to recondition yourself. It's time to teach yourself a new response.

Practice the ownership game daily. After a while, you'll get into the habit. Just as Pavlov's dogs automatically salivated at the sound of a bell, you'll automatically respond to situations by taking ownership. Best of all, you'll develop the habit of taking ownership in all aspects of your life, not only at work, but in your personal relationships, at home, with friends, with strangers in line at the grocery store—in all your interactions.

You'll also learn to take ownership of your frame of mind. Why leave your attitude up to chance? Instead of adopting whatever random mood strikes you, you could choose "upness": enthusiasm, optimism, and alertness. Nobody could possibly feel cheerful and optimistic all the time, but with practice, you can make upness your default mode of operation, the mental state you return to whenever you take a moment to refocus.

Just like that well-polished first set of wheels, your attitude is all yours. Drive it with pride.

> Taking ownership can mean taking responsibility for finding a creative solution to a problem. Once we scheduled a luncheon meeting in a conference room only to find that the room was packed with boxes of equipment, leaving no room on the tables. One of our staff, Jan Miner-Kane, said, "We'll just have to have a carpet picnic." And we did. We spread everything out on the

floor picnic-style. The unusual arrangement gave the whole lun-cheon a delightful feel of spontaneity.

Own Your Actions and Attitude

- You can fix mistakes and overcome failures.
- You have the power to repair damaged relationships.
- You experience a surge of potency and a sense of pride.
- You'll never again be a victim of circumstance.

CHAPTER 14

Key Catalyst: Stay Flexible

Get off what's not working. Shift perspectives. Maintain
the ability to change what you are doing to get the
outcome you desire.

What You'll Discover in This Chapter:

- How to live with change
- How to recognize when something's not working
- A little perk all risk-takers enjoy

When you're through changing, you're through.
—*Bruce Barton*

Go on. Make a change. Odds are you'll thank yourself for it later.

People in their eighties and nineties, approaching the final years of their long lives, tell us their regrets are more often about the opportunities for change they *didn't* take than the ones they did. Change—calculated change—pays off more often than not. Hockey player Wayne Gretzky put it this way: "You miss 100 percent of the goals you never try for."

Then why don't people make more changes? What keeps people from trying new things? Comfort. Convenience. Fear of the unknown. Using old methods *feels* easier—even though it often isn't.

Once you've determined it's time to change, how do you decide on a new course of action?

You become a seeker. This is the fun part. It's like embarking on an adventure. You're on a quest for new ideas, new methods, new approaches.

How well do you handle change? Do you chafe against it? Do you latch onto old ways of doing things, even when you know they don't work? We all do sometimes. It's not easy to recognize or admit when something isn't working. Some people routinely fight against change. You've probably known rigid, inflexible people who refuse to adapt to new circumstances. But let me ask you, how many *highly successful* rigid people do you know?

What's flexibility? It's the capability to respond or conform to new or changing situations to obtain the outcome you want. It's the ability to get off what's not working and find what *does* work. And it's another prime ingredient of a successful life in a changing world.

At SuperCamp we teach that FEAR stands for Forecasted Expectations that Appear Real. We're terrified of what might happen if we speak in front of a group, jump off the pole, make a big change, and so forth. But really, what *is* going to happen? Nothing that justifies that level of dread. When you commit yourself to doing something worthwhile in spite of your fear—when you commit to make changes to achieve the outcome—the fear vanishes and you move right through.

I once attended a self-development workshop in which the teacher asked us to name our top three fears. I told him mine were enclosed spaces, being chased by dogs, and my mom being mad at me. He said, "Notice when these happen."

Within the next month, all three of those scenarios came to me. I got stuck in an elevator. On the way to a meeting, I was confronted by three angry dogs that mysteriously turned and ran away moments before they reached me. And my sister called to say our mom was mad at me for not being more open with her.

As soon as each fear came up, I thought, "Oh, there's that one." And I moved through it. It's not the facing of the fears that's frightening; it's only the *anticipation* of those fearful events that causes discomfort, whether they happen or not. When you focus on the outcome, not the fear, you can move right through it.

Why Flexibility?

Every day, you face situations that are different from what you'd planned. You have a choice: you can either be rigid and stick with a set of behaviors that no longer fit the plan, or you can adapt and handle them with flexibility.

My mom's birthday was January first, and she hated it. People always seemed to feel obligated to make every New Year's party they invited her to a partial birthday celebration. Finally, she decided she'd had enough and "changed" her birthday to August twenty-fifth, my dad's birthday. Then they could celebrate together. Problem solved. Simple as that. I loved the flexibility in that decision: Don't like your birthday? Change it! Who's to say you can't?

> I learned a valuable lesson about flexibility during the early days of my first marriage. I had grown up in one neighborhood, but I married a man who worked for Hyatt Hotels and transferred to a different location every other year. Like clockwork, every two years, we'd uproot and move. With every move, things changed: my lifestyle, my personal habits, even my waking times. I learned to use those moves to mark changes in my life, like chapters in a book. I even used a move to stop smoking. I had started in high school because most of my friends smoked—in the days before the dangers of smoking were widely known. We moved from Albany to Chicago, and I smoked my last cigarette on the plane (you could smoke on planes back then). I put out my last cigarette just before the plane's wheels touched down and never smoked another one.

Life refuses to conform to a plan. It's fluid, dynamic, ever-changing. Staying flexible means having the courage and openness to change with it.

Every aspect of our lives demands flexibility. You're running six mornings a week to train for a tennis tournament but you sprain your ankle; instead of giving up, you swim in the mornings until you heal. You've planned lunch with an old friend at a swanky bistro, but when you learn that she's bringing her four small kids, you opt instead for lunch at Burgerama, where they've got a play place. You're planting a bed of red roses and need six more to finish, but your local nursery is out of the red variety; you opt to alternate red with white. You get the promotion of a lifetime, but at the same time your mother falls ill; you defer your job change for six months so you can take care of her, while training two evenings a week for your new position. Life can require flexibility of you in the greatest and smallest of situations.

Life also demands flexibility if you're trying to get better at what you do. Life abhors a steady state: if you're not seeking to improve, you backslide. Flexibility challenges you to let go of what's not working and try new things until you hit upon what does work.

Be Ready to Change What You're Doing to Reach Your Goals

It's hard to recognize and even harder to admit when something's not working. You've invested time, money, pride—you've convinced yourself it has to work. To become flexible, develop the ability to recognize when it's time to let go of an outmoded method and try something new. It's hard on the ego, but until you admit you've got a problem, you can't take the next step.

To start, you have to accept the reality of change. Recognize that it's normal to change the way you do things because circumstances change. It's nothing personal—it's just the nature of life. The best plans in the world can become obsolete. Make it okay for something not to work.

Second, in order to let go of things that aren't working, learn to detach your ego. We get our pride wrapped up in our methods; we take the need for change as a personal indictment against our intelligence and our integrity. Or sometimes we just get stubbornly attached to our way of doing things because it's "our way." Get your ego out of your method so that it doesn't get in the way of your flexibility. Save ego for the results, not the means. Take your work, not yourself, seriously. What you want is more important than looking good.

Third, suspend your assumptions. In order to see when change is needed, you have to become conscious of your beliefs about a given situation. Don't judge alternate paths before you've tried them. To suspend assumptions, you have to recognize them. To recognize them, you have to become a rigorous questioner of your own thoughts, beliefs, and feelings. Question authority! Learn to ask yourself, "Why do I think that?"

Finally, learn to recognize the difference between a plan that's not working and a temporary setback. When things are going badly, it could be because the method is bad and doomed to fail, or it may simply be a momentary downtick on a massive upswing. How will you know the difference? Your gut will tell you. Tune in to your gut, then stop and measure your results.

> Steve Arrowood, SuperCamp manager, told me, "I had an epiphany driving to work today that every single reason, every single time that I get upset, frustrated, or angry, is because I am not truly flexible in thought. I expected things or people to be a certain way, they weren't, and I had trained my brain to respond with that negative emotion. I am not yet flexible in those moments. When I learn to become at peace with outcomes and occurrences that are different than my own mind's expectations, then I will be much more ready to adapt and respond with effectiveness when things don't go 'right.'"

Jump into the Unknown: Explore Alternative Paths

New ideas don't come to those with closed minds. When it's time to reformulate your actions, break yourself wide open. Start by promising yourself to be open to new thoughts. Learn to suspend your assumptions and listen without judgment. Brainstorm. Branch out. Get creative. Explore as many possible solutions as you can. By throwing yourself open to the possibilities, you'll discover avenues for success that you would never have considered before. You might even find ways to improve things that *are* working.

Ask other people for their opinions—not just experts in that particular subject, but anyone whose opinion you respect. Borrow paradigms from other subjects, other applications. If you can find wisdom in the way a violin is tuned, that same method may apply to the way an annual report is written. If the patrol method Canadian geese use to safeguard their flocks works for them, the same method might work to keep a group of nine-year-olds safe on a camping trip. Be willing to cross borders, mix and match, move methods from one application to another, and stand them on their heads.

Don't fall back into rigidity once you've found a possible solution. If the old method wasn't *the* method, this new one might not be it, either. Be ready to try several options. Assign a deadline to the experiment and give it all you've got for the duration. If, in that time, it yields few results, let it go.

If you want to experience whole-life Quantum Success, learn to dance with change. To succeed, you have to look for ways to make *everything* better. Suspend your assumptions, seek new ground, throw yourself headlong into the unknown.

Complacency is the enemy of success. When you get comfortable, you stop moving forward. You dig in, shut down, doze off, disengage. Your spirit falls asleep.

If complacency is success's enemy, change is its exasperating best friend. Change wakes you up, gets you on your feet, and engages you.

Change for its own sake isn't what I'm talking about here. It doesn't work to simply change things randomly. There are some people who routinely mess things up even when they're going well. The rule of thumb when it comes to change is to keep what's working; let go of what's not.

When you commit to living in change, you'll discover a side benefit: life's more fun this way. Rising to meet the unknown can be a thrill. A friend who's president of a state university told me he knows he's on track, moving things forward, when he feels a bit of fear. Check yourself: are you at times tingling with fear? Do you feel as though you're riding the deck of a pitching ship? Are you experiencing that heightened sense of alertness and readiness that comes with facing change? Excellent! That's how you know you've entered the undiscovered country where Quantum Success is possible.

Staying Flexible Leads You to Discovery

- You can let go of what's not working.
- You can detach your ego from the plan.
- You can break yourself open and seek out new alternatives.
- Risk takers have more fun; they live in a state of heightened awareness and greater excitement.

CHAPTER 15

Key Catalyst:
Keep Your Balance

Create balance in your life by apportioning your time
according to your highest priorities.

What You'll Discover in This Chapter:

- How to keep from feeling as though some part of life is
  passing you by
- How to recognize when your life is out of balance
- Why balance isn't about apportioning equal time, but about
  examining priorities

The antidote to exhaustion is wholeheartedness.
It's the things you do half-heartedly that really wear you out.
—David Whyte

Keeping your balance is all about bringing your life into alignment, recognizing when some part of your life doesn't reflect your priorities, and arranging your life in a way that creates an ongoing sense of peace and fulfillment.

Balance is the subtlest of the 8 Key Catalysts. You may not always recognize it when it's there, but you'll feel its absence. Imbalance clanks loudly, like an out-of-tune piano. When you're out of balance, you know it. And so does everyone around you.

Fulfillment brings a sense of balance, a quiet peace. When the elements of your life are in balance, you're able to make time for what matters, even if you're extremely busy—and what successful person isn't? When you're fulfilled, you're not plagued with the nagging sensation that some aspect of life is passing you by. When we began developing the 8 Key Catalysts, I first took balance to mean you had to devote equal time and energy to all the relevant aspects of your life. I made a pie chart and devoted equal slices to work, home, family, friends, charitable organizations, and so forth, and then set about trying to apportion my time to match the chart. No matter how hard I tried to do that, no matter how close I got to that goal, something still felt out of whack. Something was lacking in integrity. I came to realize that it wasn't a matter of slavishly devoting equal time, but of finding the allotment of time and energy that creates the greatest sense of fulfillment. Of course, I do face situations where I don't choose to give my full attention, but I do choose to pay attention to what's important to me. It wasn't necessary to give equal time down to the minute; but it was vital, when I was giving time to something or someone, to give my full attention. That's balance.

Why Balance?

The first symptom that your life is out of balance may be the sensation that you're missing something. Later, the vacuum caused by that "something missing" begins to affect your performance in other areas of your life. Burnout, frustration, exhaustion, disillusionment, emptiness, and fatigue are all symptoms of imbalance. In extreme imbalance, your life flies apart. You become unable to function. You collapse. You self-destruct.

The biggest casualty in loss of balance is the big picture. The further out of whack your life gets, the harder it is to stay focused on the reasons you're doing all these things in the first place. You can't be the sparkling, radiant "higher you" when the things that are important to you aren't getting the attention they need. Lose your balance, and you lose your dream.

When you make sufficient time for the things that matter, even when it means adjusting your routine from time to time or doing things a little differently than planned, you're able to stay focused on the big picture. You're able to commit yourself for the long haul.

Alignment brings peace and renewal. When you're in balance, you experience a quiet sense of well-being. In that place of inner peace you'll find that the big picture becomes visible again.

> SuperCamp manager Steve Arrowood defines four components that support balance in mind, body, and spirit.
>
> • Family and friends
> • Being in the zone
> • Measuring yourself (rather than comparing yourself to others)
> • Forgiving
>
> Research shows that having these four components in your life brings fulfillment and a sense of balance and happiness.

Take Personal Time—Especially When You Can Least Afford It

Odds are, you won't recognize you're out of balance unless you take time off to step back from your life for a little while. And as luck would have it, the times you're most in need of that perspective are often the times when it's most difficult to stop long enough to gain it.

Not long ago, I found myself doing more traveling than usual. For several months at a stretch, I was zigzagging across the country and leapfrogging overseas, attending conferences and speaking engagements. I'd dash home in between events to spend time with my family. Sometimes I'd be home long enough to wash a few clothes, then I'd be off again. I spent a week at Disneyland with my grandchildren and loved it, even though I knew I'd be getting on the plane again the following Saturday. I felt nourished by being with my family, but I also knew I was overdoing it. So I planned some personal time when I returned from my next trip. Even a short moment can bring back the balance.

Your body and spirit will tell you what they need, even if your conscious mind is too frenzied to hear them. Life seldom proceeds at an even pace. You have to stay aware of how you're responding to given situations.

Balance has little to do with the *amount* of time you spend. When I'm focused and excited about something, I can spend mega hours at it and feel fulfilled and balanced. I never worry about whether I'm spending too much time at something. Of course, people with a spouse or young children, who have committed their time, have to stay aware of whether they're fulfilling that commitment—they don't have the luxury of putting unlimited amounts of time into another venture. But the secret to balance lies not in an allotment of time but in an awareness of your priorities.

Check Your Priorities Daily

When you're driving a car, you're making constant small corrections. You're aligning the wheel and adjusting the gas almost automatically. Keeping your life in balance requires the same kind of ongoing correction process. Balance is about choices. When you're keeping yourself in balance, you're making a thousand internal corrections each day. You're constantly asking yourself, "What do I value? What's really important? Does this activity really need to be done now?"

Your balancing act will often require you to choose one valued activity over another. Keep your balance by compensating for that choice at another time. You can't compete in that chess tournament and spend time with your kids in the same afternoon; since the tournament time is fixed and the "kid time" isn't, go to the tournament in the day and take the kids to the movies that night.

No matter how good you become at it, you won't be in balance every moment of every day. Tune into the signals your mind, spirit, and body send that warn you when you're slipping out of balance. Compensate sooner rather than later. The quicker you realign yourself, the smaller the "wobble" you'll have to correct.

The balance that comes from fulfillment acts as a lens. It clears the view to your dream. Balance and the big picture are self-reinforcing energies. Stay balanced, and you'll be able to keep the big picture in sight; stay focused on the big picture, and you'll see clearly the choices that will keep your balance.

Fulfillment creates balance. Tune in to what fulfills you. Make choices that are consistent with what makes you feel fulfilled.

The Balancing Act

- Success saturates. Practice and learning in one area makes you better in all areas.
- When you think you're too busy to rest—it's time to rest.
- Give the things that matter the amount of time and energy that creates the greatest sense of fulfillment.

PART IV

Speed Your Ride with Key Adaptability Skills

When you're following your passion, people take notice. They're attracted to you. Your radiance draws them and inspires them. By courageously living up to the highest possible vision of yourself, you show others what their own lives could be.

When you move to your own vision, when you keep true to your inner guidance system and you apply the 8 Key Catalysts, your dream unfolds to serve those around you. There's an integrity, a purpose, a deep-down *rightness* in your actions.

When you're living your dream, people will also sense about you a thirst for knowledge, feedback, and a love of learning. It comes with the territory. People in the midst of a radiant explosion are expanding outward, acquiring new information, gaining new insights and experiences. They know that they'll be able to adopt whatever information they acquire to catapult themselves forward.

If you and your dream are going to survive and thrive in the twenty-first century, you'll need to develop an adaptive mind that uses your whole brain in new and expansive ways. No matter how powerful your dream or how solid your character, you can't realize much of your vision if you're not able to adapt to the realities of your world. We live in an era of massive change and torrential information. To seek Quantum Success in that maelstrom requires you to be a master of knowledge acquisition and a fast adapter.

That's what you're about to become.

Within the next four chapters, you'll discover techniques for using both sides of your brain to acquire and process new information quickly, deeply, and thoroughly. You'll understand your natural behavior style and be able to look at almost anything from four different perspectives. You'll learn how to think creatively, cross-pollinate ideas, and solve problems at a higher level. You'll maximize the awesome power of your memory to retain information more completely and recall it rapidly. And you'll develop a response system that will allow you to adapt deftly to changing circumstances.

Most of the adaptability methods you're about to learn aren't new—I didn't invent them. But I've put them together in a strategy that's tailor-made for the successful twenty-first century individual. These techniques don't just help you get by; they help you get ahead. They turn rapid change and mass information from deterrents into assets.

Welcome to the most dynamic element of Quantum Success.

CHAPTER 16

Understand Behavior and Learning Styles

Which side of your brain do you favor? Are you an orderly, factual left-brainer, or an intuitive, global right-brainer? What is your natural behavior style? Are you a down-to-earth, hands-on leader? Do you have a fiery nature, inspiring others with flair and energy? Are you easily moved to tears, yet flow calmly keeping others in check? Or is your head in the clouds with thoughts and theories? Identifying your preferred behavior style, and those of the people in your life will help you become a more effective learner—and a better communicator.

What You'll Discover in This Chapter:

- How to acquire left-brain knowledge if you're a right-brain person, and right-brain knowledge if you're a left-brain person
- Your natural behavior style—and how it gives you an edge
- How to communicate with people whose learning styles are different than yours
- How to make your level of understanding skyrocket

Fuller

A great deal of miscommunication comes down to a difference in information-processing styles. One person asks a question on one wavelength; the other person answers on another. For example, you might ask a family member how cold it is outside because you want to decide on wearing a jacket or a sweater. He may hear you the way he processes information and give you the exact temperature—fifty-five degrees—which doesn't tell you how it "feels," which is what you really want to know. People with different behavior and learning styles often struggle to understand one another. When you're aware of your own personal style of seeking and acquiring information, you'll have a better understanding of the way to ask for the information you're seeking. And when you know the behavior and learning styles of those around you, you'll be better prepared to interact with them in a way that increases their comprehension—for example, "Is it sweater weather or jacket weather?"

Keep in mind that when I say "styles," I'm talking in generalizations. No single behavior style can possibly capture the sum total of an individual. Styles are guidelines only. They're characterizations, not definitions. Use them only to the extent that they help you learn and communicate better.

How Does It Help to Identify Learning Styles?

When you understand learning styles, you know how you learn best, and you can arrange incoming information to create a direct feed to your brain. You can acquire new knowledge quickly because you're putting it into the kinds of chunks your brain is configured to accept.

Your understanding skyrockets when you match your acquisition activities with your strongest learning style. Less information gets by you; more information is at your command. Behavioral researchers have amassed piles of data to support this. Knowing your best learning style and how to apply it allows you to take charge of your own learning.

But there's more. When you harness the power of your own personal learning style, your communication becomes more effective. When you are able to identify your own behavior and learning acquisition style, and the styles of others, you'll be able to head off miscommunication because you'll have a better idea of how to present information to yourself and others. And you know from reading the previous chapters why communication is important: it's the universal relationship fuel. Communication grows relationships; relationships grow success.

Tailor Your Learning to Your Learning Style

Most of us are stronger in one learning style than another. When you know how you learn best, and you're aware of your weaknesses, you can create the learning experience that suits you best.

To give you an example of how this works, let's look at one easy system for categorizing styles of learning: VAK. VAK stands for Visual, Auditory, and Kinesthetic (movement/touch/emotion). The VAK theory says an individual may be a strong or weak learner in any one of these areas. If you're primarily a visual learner, you learn best when you see information to process it fully. If you're a strong auditory learner, you learn best when you hear it, and if you're a kinesthetic learner, you learn best with hands-on experience. If you're weak in any one of these areas, you'll have trouble with certain kinds of learning, and you'll learn best if you come up with ways to reinforce your knowledge acquisition.

I'm a low-auditory learner. When I was in school I had trouble learning languages. It was a mystery to me how they seemed to come so effortlessly to other people. In high school, I was trying to master Spanish. I'd hear it spoken and try to repeat it. I just couldn't get it to stick. But when I tried writing out the words and making myself a set of flash cards to go with the lessons, I started getting somewhere. Both the kinesthetic activity of forming the words with my hands and the visual reference that the written words created bolstered my auditory weakness.

If I hadn't known my own learning style, strengths, and weaknesses, I probably wouldn't have hit upon the solution.

Experience Before Label

In Quantum Learning we teach "Experience Before Label." Real-time, real-world, firsthand concrete learning experiences provide the strongest concept development and understanding for both children and adults. After the experience, we make the learner conscious of the new knowledge gained by "labeling" it, naming, explaining, and connecting the experience and the lesson. The power is in providing the students an experience first. It minimizes the preconceived notions and stereotypes that can interfere with learning and makes understanding stronger.

Right Brain, Left Brain: Which Should You Get to Know Better?

The choices you make, the activities and people you prefer, and the way you perceive the world have a lot to do with whether you favor the left or right hemisphere of your brain. Are you

predominately a left-brainer? People who favor the left hemispheres of their brains tend to be logical, sequential, and highly
structured. They make great accountants, engineers, and admin-
istrators. Or are you mostly a right-brainer? Right-brain thinkers
are global, emotional, intuitive, and often highly sociable. They're
artists, teachers, and nurturers.

Most people learn better with the side of the brain they favor.
Left-brainers absorb facts and figures with ease, but they have
trouble marshalling "fuzzier" knowledge like aesthetics and emotions. Right-brainers pick up on emotions, moods, and aesthetic
nuances, but turn off in the face of cold equations and dry facts.

Just recognizing which side of the brain you favor will help
you identify which areas will prove easy for you to acquire knowledge and understanding in and which may present a challenge.
But the real masters of knowledge acquisition aren't content to
learn with only half a brain. The best learners learn with *both*
sides of their brains. You can teach yourself to do this. You can
strengthen the weaker side of your brain and foster connections
between the two hemispheres.

Your brain changes to accommodate your thought patterns.
Parts of your brain that you use frequently get stronger; parts that
fall into disuse get weaker. If you're mostly a right-brainer, you
can strengthen your left-brain acquisition by practicing left-brain
activities that involve numbers, order, logic, and facts. If you're primarily a left-brainer, you can build up the connections in your
right brain by exposing yourself to the arts.

If you're a right-brainer, take up chess; if you're a left-brainer,
paint with watercolors. Best of all, adopt a hobby that forces you
to use both sides of your brain at once, like music, which is both
mathematical and aesthetic, or poker, which involves mathematical computations and an eye for emotional expression.

The TetraMap of Nature: Find Your Natural Behavior Style

You're about to look at your own behavior from a new perspective. You're also going to discover a few things about the behaviors of the people who have the greatest impact on your dream. But first, what Element describes you best?

Your Behavior: What Element Describes You?

Your personality, experience, education, and thinking style draw you to a particular element. Each of the four Elements is characterized by certain inclinations and learning preferences. Know your Element, and you'll know more about the way you learn. Identify others' preferred Elements, and you'll understand why they fit perfectly into certain circumstances, and seem out of place in others.

TetraMap™ was developed by Yoshimi and Jon Brett of New Zealand. The Bretts have been developing, researching, implementing, and integrating the four traditional elements into their work for more than twenty years. In the 1990s they had a serendipitous encounter with Buckminster Fuller's great works, including his use of the tetrahedron. Bucky believed that the tetrahedron was at the root of all natural human behavior. It has a sense of equality and interconnectedness, like human beings. TetraMap became the perfect new-millennium model to apply the four traditional elements to the holistic, synergistic, interdependent world of human beings.

I've come to rely on TetraMap as a powerful guide to understanding behavior and learning preferences. It's an all-encompassing system that accommodates models that date back to Hippocrates in 450 BC and more current models you may have experienced, like Marston's DISC, or Myers Briggs.

In the Bretts' book, *TetraMap: How to Develop People & Business the Way Nature Intended* (Learnology, 2002), they further demonstrate how the four Elements relate to these other models, and how they correspond to left and right brain hemispheres. Earth and Air tend to be left-hemisphere people; Fire and Water tend to favor the right hemisphere. TetraMap focuses you on valuing uniqueness while learning to adapt to different points of view.

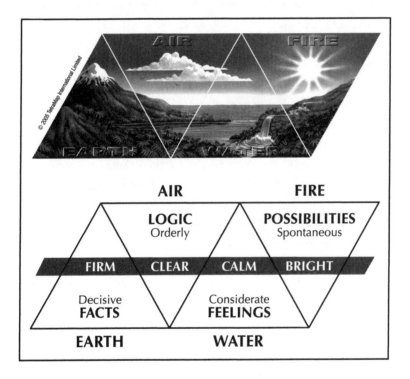

The TetraMap is liberating for those who grasp how nature's basic elements, Earth, Air, Water, and Fire, are metaphors for behavior. It helps us appreciate what others bring to a situation, and to respect their natural behavior.

How Do You Recognize the Behavior Style of Others?

Once you know the Elements of the people in your life, you'll find it easier to understand how they learn, communicate, and handle everyday situations. You'll be able to predict what environments are likely to suit them and which tasks they'll enjoy. And you will appreciate what others bring to a situation, and respect their natural behavior. Look for these characteristics in the people around you.

Earth Elements tend to rise to the top in social situations. In a group, the person leading the conversation or activity is likely an Earth. They're also highly competitive. Do you know someone who turns everything into a contest? People who belong to other Elements might even call the Earth bossy or arrogant. The Earth is strongly driven. The person who stands out as highly motivated is likely an Earth.

Air Elements are the people you count on to get things done—particularly the detail-oriented tasks. You can't necessarily tell Airs by their socializing; an Air may be an introvert or an extrovert, though many are quite content to squirrel away and work by themselves for hours. Air Elements love order. Do you know somebody who gets upset when you move things around on her desk? She's probably an Air.

Fire Elements are the people who inspire you—or drive you crazy—or both. A Fire can be admired for his genius or dismissed as a fruit loop. Fires march to their own drummers. Do you know someone who's brimming with new ideas? Someone who loves change? If all else fails, identify the Fire by his boundless enthusiasm. Fires do things with great passion.

During one vision day, the staff got into groups by Element. They discussed how they liked to interact and how they liked others to communicate to them. It got very emotional, because the Fires felt others didn't take them or their ideas seriously, just because they had so much fun planning and brainstorming. The exercise turned into a major discussion with lots of tears.

Water Elements are easy to identify—who's the magpie in the group? Who spends the most time talking? Who's the one everybody feels comfortable going to with problems? When you find yourself at ease in conversation with someone, you're likely talking to a Water.

How Do the Different Behavior Styles Interact?

I'm Earth with strong Fire characteristics; my husband Joe is also an Earth, but with Air attributes. We're both conscious of each other's natural tendency to lead, so we sometimes end up deferring to one another—a lot. Many of our days together sound like this:

"What do you want to do today?"

"Whatever you want to do."

"But what do *you* want to do?"

Elements in alignment can sometimes happily lead each other down a path to nowhere. They can agree too much and miss the bigger picture. At other times they can support each other in accomplishing great things. But *differing* Elements can bring a multifaceted perspective to a group effort.

You've heard the phrase "agree to disagree?" Well, I don't agree. When you gloss over the places of disagreement, you miss some of the best chances for creative solutions and innovative ideas. If you see the places where you differ as strengths rather than problem areas, you open up whole new possibilities. The trick to doing this lies in respecting the ways different behavior Elements interact.

As you saw in the example of "sweater weather or jacket weather," people with different behavior Elements communicate differently. Once you recognize a particular Element, you can adapt the way you communicate with that person to maximize the flow of information.

The intent is to improve communication and relationships by responding more appropriately to the behavior of others. It's a model of behavior, not people. People are much more complex than just their behavior.

When communicating with Earth Elements, give them information quickly, clearly, and precisely. Have the facts ready. Give it to them in a logical sequence. Don't jump around; get to the point. Earth Elements often go ballistic when conversations turn confrontational. If you get into an argument with an Earth, keep your cool. If you anticipate a conflict, practice the conversation ahead of time.

I once divided my staff into groups based on their Elements and asked them, "What's fun about this organization?" The Earths' response: meetings, talks about the future, baseball games, and our presentations on our most embarrassing moments.

Talking to Air Elements means treading lightly on emotional ground. They hate conflict, and don't express their feelings comfortably. When giving Airs information, stick to the facts, particularly in writing, which is the communication method they prefer.

When asked what was most fun about our organization, Airs said they liked the contests and the community service best.

Communicating with Waters is a breeze, as long as the subject is feelings or people. Acknowledge feelings, but gently guide them back to the problem at hand. Help them prioritize; give them deadlines. Waters don't like making unpopular decisions, so help them find a win–win scenario whenever possible.

During the group exercise, the Waters said the most fun things about our organization were bringing their kids to work, blowing bubbles, laughing, pet day, and dinner cruises—the social stuff.

If you can get a word in edgewise with Fire Elements, show some enthusiasm; they're more likely to listen. Listen patiently to a Fire, and she'll be more likely to listen to you. Repeat and rephrase what Fires say to make sure you follow them. Prepare thoroughly in advance for a confrontation with a Fire; they're highly persuasive arguers.

What did the Fire Elements like best about our company? Friday wind-downs, beach days, and public acknowledgment.

Of course, no one style of approach or communication will work all the time. That's because we all have aspects of all four Elements in different degrees. Our second preferred style may make all the difference to a situation, depending on the subject, the stress levels, the current state, or the individual. The most important step is to practice flexibility in approaching and communicating with all the Elements.

Take a moment to consider again the four Elements within each of us. The firmness and stability of Earth, the clarity and all-knowingness of Air, the calm and compassion of Water, and the brightness and inspiration of Fire. Perspectives from all four Elements add depth and meaning to our interactions and endeavors.

Do You Know These People?

External Focus (Earth & Fire)
Act quickly, interested in outcomes.
Focus on others' behavior.

Internal Focus (Air & Water)
Think before acting, interested in process.
Focus on affecting own behavior.

Left-Brain (Earth & Air)
Natural with numbers, languages, and logic.
Task-oriented, good at organizing others.

Right-Brain (Water & Fire)
Natural with patterns, color, and intuition.
People-oriented, good at enrolling others.

Abstract/Conceptual Base (Air & Fire)
Known for their up-in-the-air ideas, theories,
and perceptions.

Concrete/Practical Base (Earth & Water)
Known for their down-to-earth deeds and
common sense.

The synergy of the elements in nature creates beauty and life itself. They allow us to create more than we ever would alone.

By all means, know your own greatest strength and the strengths of those around you. But don't track yourself or others exclusively by strong points. The best players are those who bring an entire range of talents to the game. Although people generally learn best in situations that suit their dominant behavior Element, they have secondary strengths as well. A Fire might make an excellent writer, but if she wants to be a professional, she has to learn how to interview like a Water, proofread her work with the quiet rigor of an Air, and move her career upward like an Earth. A great mom or dad may be primarily an Earth, but because managing a family is such a multifaceted task, it certainly helps parents to learn how to solve problems creatively the way Fires do, and how to network with other families, the way Waters can. And a world-class triathlete, full of the competitive ambition of the Earth, will need some of the Air's grasp of routine and habit to complete her training, along with some of the Fire's knack for long-range planning to reach the peak of her abilities.

Give yourself, and the people in your life, opportunities to be out of their comfort zone sometimes. If you're a Fire, create some Air-like routine niches in your life where your job is to quietly take orders and calmly carry them out. Give a Water the helm from time to time so that he has a chance to build some Earth-like management muscles. Let a left-brain person pursue opportunities to develop her creative right-brain side. Play to strengths, but don't pass up opportunities to strengthen weaker areas.

Behavior and Learning Styles

- Quantum learners are strong in both brain hemispheres. They choose activities that strengthen the weaker side.

- Your learning style shows you how you acquire knowledge and process information.
- Know your behavior and learning style, and you'll know how to arrange your learning and interactions for maximum effectiveness.
- Know the behavior styles of those around you, and you'll enhance the effectiveness of your communication.

CHAPTER 17

Make Visual
Connections

If you want to acquire information deeply and
thoroughly, if you want to retrieve it quickly and
accurately, and if you want to apply it creatively, teach
yourself to acquire it with your whole brain—
with both hemispheres learning simultaneously,
coordinating their efforts.

What You'll Discover in This Chapter:

- How to get both hemispheres of your brain in on learning,
  planning, and problem solving
- How to train your mind to pay attention (even in boring
  situations)
- How to get more fun out of owning a brain

The bottom line is a learning curve.
—Nancy Margulies

Brains are fun. If you're accustomed to messing around with your brain—tackling puzzles, conundrums, and memory challenges, teasing out rhymes and double entendres from conversations, making outrageous connections between unrelated items, seeking out new experiences, and dancing on the edge of the absurd—then you know how neat it is to have a brain of your very own to play with. And if you're accustomed to placing new challenges before your brain, then you're probably ahead of the game when it comes to learning, because odds are you're using a more balanced proportion of both sides of your brain.

Having fun with your gray matter makes you a better learner. Richard Restak, MD, author of *The New Brain: How the Modern Age Is Rewiring Your Mind* (Rodale, 2003), says your brain changes every day. Your brain has an enormous capacity for change. Its structure and function is not fixed. Just a few years ago, scientists still believed that the brain's plasticity (capacity for change) largely ceased by adolescence. Now we know that our brains never lose the power to transform themselves on the basis of experience.

In the last chapter you gained a better understanding of the way your brain processes information. You saw how the two hemispheres of your brain function differently, and how the hemisphere you favor predisposes you to a certain personality type and learning style. You discovered that by catering to that preference you could learn faster and deeper.

Now, instead of leaning on your strengths, we're going to take the road less traveled. We're going to get *both* sides of your brain in on the action, both the hemisphere you favor and the one you use less frequently. You're the master of your brain. You can take ownership of your thought processes and strengthen the areas where you're not as strong.

You'll also learn how to apply a number of practical acquisition techniques that engage both sides of your brain at the same time.

Why Whole-Brain Acquisition?

Why strive to acquire information with your whole brain? Because the more of your brain you engage in the process, the more deeply you'll retain the information. You'll not only learn more facets of the information, you'll also be able to apply it creatively—and you'll be able to discover more meaning in it.

Get Both Hemispheres of Your Brain in on Learning

You acquire knowledge best when you:
- Reinforce what you're learning several different ways (words with pictures, images with phrases, and so forth)
- Associate it with prior learning
- Use more than one of your five senses
- See personal importance in what you're learning.

Map with Your Mind: Sketch a Central Idea and Branch Outward

Want to give both sides of your brain a fun, creative workout—and gain some insight into something you're planning at the same time? You may have heard of a powerful whole-brain technique called Mind Mapping®. Tony Buzan developed Mind Mapping in the 1960s, and it's been catching on worldwide ever since. Mind Mapping engages both sides of the brain simultaneously.

It combines pictures, symbols, random ordering, and other right-hemisphere activities with words, logic, sequences, and other left-hemisphere activities.

Mind Mapping is great for planning events, organizing new information, capturing memories, solving problems—the applications are limitless. I've been introducing this technique for years and I'm still thrilled when I hear people tell me they Mind Mapped their upcoming vacation, holiday dinner, or kid's birthday party. Mind Mapping feels like a cross between doodling and note-taking, only it's a lot more fun than either. You'll be amazed at the way your mind processes information when you play with this whole-brain technique.

How do you acquire information with Mind Mapping? First, I want you to think about the way you're accustomed to writing down information. In a classroom or meeting, or when you're taking notes from a book, how do you proceed? You might make an orderly column of words, carefully numbered, with a black ballpoint pen, or perhaps you make a messy scribble that even you have trouble deciphering later. Whatever the case, you're about to add something new to your method.

Gather up some colored pencils and a large piece of paper. Then think of a subject: a piece of learning you're trying to master, a decision you're trying to make, or an event you're trying to plan. Your next vacation? The last book you read? For starters, pick a subject that draws you—now *you're* going to draw *it*. I've included my Mind Map of Quantum Success in developing stages as a reference.

Turn the paper horizontally so you'll have more room to branch out. Now make your Mind Map.

Put your main topic in the center of the page, whether it's a written word, a drawing, or both. If you can work a drawing in somehow, you'll make the experience more powerful. A drawing is a stronger way to reinforce a central idea than a mere word or phrase.

Draw a branch that flows from thick to thin, like the branches of a tree, extending from the main idea for each subtopic and key point. Make each branch a different color or rotate colors to keep it varied. Don't use the same color for two branches side by side; the varied colors help you distinguish between branches. Print a key word on top of each branch, one per line.

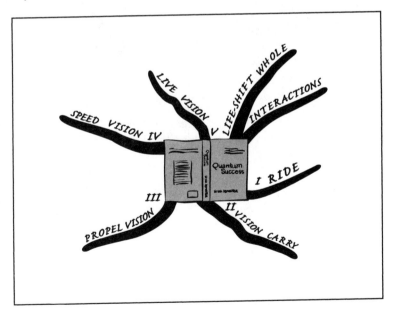

Attach new branches to your subtopics. As you remember subjects or think of new ideas, draw branches fanning out from the tips of the subtopic branches.

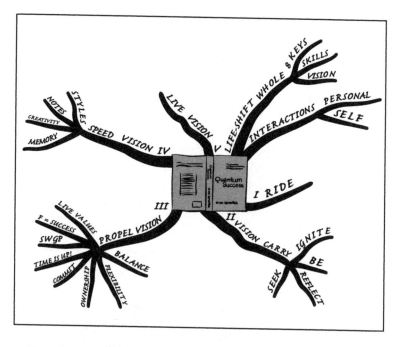

Develop your branches. Each tip of a branch can have a whole cluster of additional branches leading off of it.

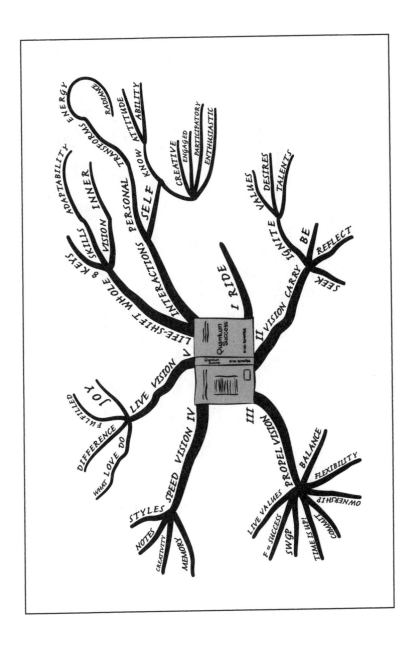

Get creative. Unleash your artistic ability—add pictures, poems, symbols, relate it to your personal experiences. Let it become a personal work of art.

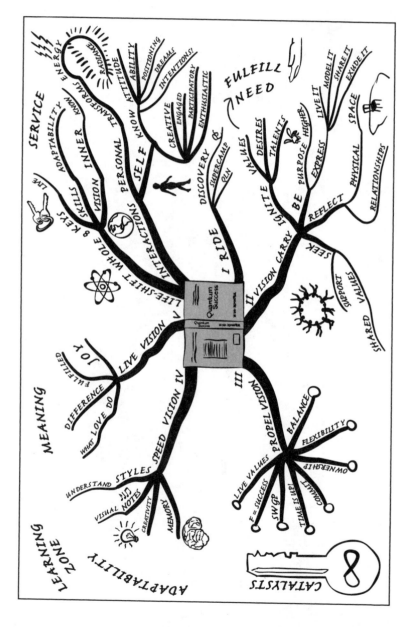

Step back and see what the finished picture tells you. Your Mind Map gives you the "big picture" of a subject, an idea, or a plan.

My Mind Map

This is the Mind Map I used to create this chapter so I could see how all the information fit together.

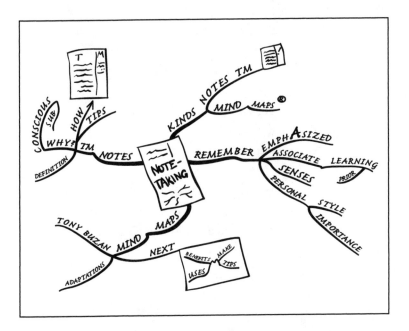

When can you use Mind Mapping? Anytime you're mastering a new subject or brainstorming a new plan. When you're starting a new writing assignment and you're not sure where to begin, use Mind Mapping to get you off and rolling. Put your topic in the center and make branches of your main points. Then use your map to organize the way you'll present your information.

I use Mind Maps when I read books. I bounce from book to book, and I keep a Mind Map growing for each book I'm into, even novels. It helps me keep the characters straight!

I also use Mind Maps to help me organize speeches. I recently gave an hour-long seminar on learning skills. I made a map of the subject and pinned it to the wall in front of me. Instead of having to refer to written pages, I had the "big picture" right there at a glance, and could focus my attention on my audience.

You'll also find Mind Maps useful for planning events. Imagine using a Mind Map as a wedding organizer or vacation planner. The map itself might become a memento of the experience.

Mind Maps are also great ways to overcome blocked thinking. They jump-start the thought process when it runs out of steam. When your mind gets blocked, try drawing empty branches flowing from your main topic. Your mind hates unfinished business, and it will automatically try to fill in missing information. Many pro writers use Mind Mapping to overcome writer's block.

What is it about Mind Mapping that makes this technique so effective? Not only does it combine words and pictures to engage both sides of the brain, it also breaks information down into smaller chunks, making it easier to manage, and it emerges spontaneously into a natural structure that makes organizing easier.

Notes TM: A Strategy for Taking and Making Notes

Acquiring new information almost always requires some form of note-taking. It's a skill everyone needs to master, yet few of us are ever taught actual note-taking techniques. In fact, most of us probably think only in terms of *taking* notes, when an equally important part of mastering new information lies in *making* notes.

When you're taking notes, you're writing down the information you want to remember.

When you're making notes, you're writing down your own thoughts and impressions about the information.

Why is it important to do both? Because associating the information with your impressions makes it more meaningful to you. The more meaningful the information, the greater your retention.

But there's another benefit to the Taking/Making technique: It keeps your mind from wandering. Has your mind ever drifted off during a meeting or a lecture? There's a reason it does that: people speak at a rate of two hundred to three hundred words per minute, and your brain can process six hundred to eight hundred words per minute. Without sufficient stimulation, your brain wanders off in search of better fare: what you'll do after the session, what you had for lunch, the talk you had with your best friend on the phone last night. Keep your mind on track by giving it more to do with the information as it comes in. Take notes and make them at the same time.

As you take notes, keep a smaller running column on the far right-hand side of the page to make notes: Use symbols, pictures, diagrams, whatever keeps your brain interested. You'll not only stay tuned into the lesson, you'll also have a far more useful collection of material to study afterward.

Notes TM: Take Them, Make Them

Note-Taking	Note-Making
KEY POINTS: text, text, text, text, text, text, text, text, text, text, text, text, text, text, text, text, text, text, text, text	Impressions ... etc., etc., etc., etc., etc., etc.
INFORMATION: text, text, text, text, text, text, text, text, text, text, text, text, text, text, text, text, text, text, text	Thoughts ... etc., etc., etc., etc., etc.
FACT: text, text, text, text, text, text, text, text, text, text, text, text, text, text, text, text, text, text, text, text	Will this really work? etc., etc., etc., etc., etc., etc., etc.
FACT: text, text, text, text, text, text, text, text, text, text, text, text, text, text, text, text, text, text, text	

The best acquisition techniques are those that make use of both sides of your brain, that tap into both your logical, sequential brain functions and your creative, free-form intuition. The techniques I've presented here are just a sampling; plenty of others are out there awaiting your discovery. As you practice and play with them, you'll probably create a few of your own.

Making Visual Connections

- Use pictures, symbols, maps, words, and colors to engage both halves of your brain in the acquisition process.
- Train your mind to pay attention by making notes as well as taking them.

CHAPTER 18

Think in Creative Ways

You're creative. We all are—though many adults have
let their creativity atrophy. The twenty-first century
demands that we awaken our creativity and keep it sharp
so that we can rise to new challenges and see and do
things in innovative ways.

What You'll Discover in This Chapter:

- Keys to reawakening your creativity
- How to keep your creativity on call
- How to nurture creativity in others
- How to solve problems creatively

Life does not consist mainly, or even largely, of facts and happenings.
It consists mainly of the storm of thoughts that is forever
blowing through one's head.
—Mark Twain

Once I was standing elbow-to-armpit with passengers at the baggage carousel at Heathrow Airport, trying to get my bags. As usual, everybody was crowding in so tightly that nobody could see their bags, making it difficult to see them unless you were up against the carousel. As I was standing there I thought, *If airports painted a line two feet out from the baggage carousels and requested that people stand behind the line until they saw their bag, everyone could grab their luggage easily.* I saw a suggestion box on the wall nearby and hastily wrote out my idea, not expecting to hear anything. Weeks later, to my surprise, I received a reply: "Thank you for your excellent suggestion. We will try it first at the smaller Gatwick Airport, and if it is successful, we will implement it at Heathrow." You never know when your creativity might make a difference.

What do you mean, you're not creative? Everyone is—or at least they have the potential to be. Creativity is a skill like any other. Develop and practice it if you want to have it on call when you need it. When we don't use our creativity regularly, it atrophies.

Young children are naturally creative. You don't have to tell a five-year-old to draw a picture of the scary dream he had last night, or a three-year old to compose a symphony on her mom's pots and pans. They just do things like this. But creativity declines sharply as children grow, and by the time they're adults it has all but vanished—unless they work to keep it.

Your creativity is alive and well inside you, even if you haven't drawn a scary dream or banged on any pots lately. I'm not saying you're the next Mozart, Botticelli, or Spielberg. There's a difference between being creative and being a master of music, art, or film. Creativity applies to more than the arts. It's the source you tap into whenever you challenge yourself to see and do things in a new way. As a child, I discovered I had little natural talent for piano-playing or ice-skating, but as I matured, I discovered that I could be very creative when it came to bringing ideas to people. Creativity amounts to inventive, fresh, unusual answers to questions and problems, the ability to look at situations in new ways, and the capacity to try doing things differently. A blog about everyday creativity, www.creativitycentral.com/blog, promotes the mantra *What if? What else? Why not?* We can get locked into trying to find the "right" answer for every solution; what we could be looking for instead is a *creative* answer. If you look at it that way, you can see that a successful person *must* be creative.

Why Creativity?

It takes creativity to face up to challenges—and today's world is loaded with them. Our economy is becoming global. Competition is growing fiercer. New technology is developing at a blistering speed. Our world is full of accelerating "newness." Rapidly changing situations need to be approached in new and innovative ways. It takes a person with boundless creativity to continuously come at life from a fresh perspective.

Change alone is a strong argument for keeping your creative muscles limber, but there's another one—an even more compelling one. Creativity is the single greatest expression of your individuality. Nobody else in this world is creative in exactly the same way you are. Your individuality is your greatest asset. And nothing says *you* like creative expression. Your creative work is you up in neon. It's pure, raw you, gifted to the world.

Develop your creativity as a means of coping with change, but also as a means of letting yourself be known, of putting your legacy out into the world.

Creativity is the ultimate expression of individuality. When asked who he sounded like during an early audition, Elvis Presley replied, "I don't sound like nobody."

> We keep a "toy box" ready at hand during all our brainstorming sessions. The box contains juggle scarves, foot bags, Zeebees (similar to soft Frisbees), and other interactive items. Once I was in a session with a group of staffers and nothing was coming. We all got out of our chairs, spread out in the room, and tossed around a bunch of Zeebees as we continued to talk. The ideas started flowing so fast we had to stop and write each down quickly as it came up so we'd remember them all.

Creativity Is a Skill—Here's How to Develop It

How do you develop your creativity? How do you put it into action?

The best way to become a creative thinker is to act like one. Let's look at the way creative people act. Creative thinkers:

- Question everything
- Generate ideas
- Seek what might work better
- Bust paradigms
- Take action

Let's look at each of these behaviors in turn.

Creative thinkers question everything. For the creative person, curiosity is a way of life. They're inquisitive, adventurous. They have to know what makes everything tick. As small children, they peeked behind the TV set to see if there were little people going in and out of the back. Show them your new palm-top, and they'll fiddle with it until they figure out how to use it—without looking at the instructions. Let them catch you putting together a new desk or barbeque grill and they'll try to help. They're great at keeping up with technical innovations and new ways of thinking about things, just by following their curious natures.

You say this doesn't sound like you? That's a choice. You can develop this ability by practice. Make it a habit to ask *why* and *how*. Challenge everything and everyone. My friend's favorite teacher in college, Arthur, was an enthusiastic aging hippie who believed passionately in free thinking. One day in class, he was driving home the lesson, thumping on the desk with a fist to emphasize his point. "Question authority!" he boomed. "Challenge authority!"

From the back of the classroom, a student yelled back, "No!" Arthur roared with laughter. His message had hit home.

Creative thinkers generate ideas. The best way to get great ideas is to generate *lots* of ideas. The more ideas you have, the greater your options. Inventor Dr. Yoshio Nakamata, holder of twenty-three hundred patents, urges creative thinkers, "Stuff your brain, keep pumping information into it. Give your brain lots of raw material. Then give it a chance to cook." Don't judge your ideas while you're gathering them; there'll be plenty of time to do that later. If you judge ideas while they're still ripening on the vine, you blight them, and they wither and die. First, pull in your harvest—make it as bountiful as possible. Then you'll be able to sort bad from good, best from better.

Creative thinkers seek what might work better. Creative thinkers don't accept things as they are. They're always looking for ways to improve situations. Management consultant Fred Pryor says creative people see what others see, "but they think what no one else thinks." Creative thinkers don't see problems, they see challenges.

Creative thinkers bust paradigms. Paradigms are necessary—we all need sets of rules and ways to frame ideas in order to function in our world. But we can become too dependent on the comfort of paradigms. Creative thinkers aren't afraid to throw away old paradigms to make room for the new. They break through perceived boundaries.

Once a matchbook company received a letter from an inventor who said, "I have an idea that will save your company $2,000 a year. If I tell it to you, and you agree that it will work, will you pay me $500?" The company, intrigued, agreed. The inventor's response: "Put the little sandpaper strip on only one side of the matchbook cover." The company happily paid the man his $500. Where is it written that the strip has to be on both sides?

Creative thinkers take action. Creative thinkers bring ideas to fruition. They use their creativity not only to inquire, gather ideas, and invent new ways of doing things, but also to create the means to carry out those ideas. They're master planners and strategizers. They're doers. They know what's needed at each step because they're aware of their surroundings, of trends and possibilities. They're test-marketers. They seek out the actions involved in bringing a plan to actuality. Not all doers are creative, but all *successful* creative people are doers.

Action is the distinguishing factor between those who merely dream and those who succeed. Back in high school my friend George was crazy about a girl who didn't care to give him the time of day. George's usual methods of getting this girl interested didn't work. He was tempted to get discouraged and give up; instead, he took creative action. At four o'clock one foggy morning, when the girl was leaving for her part-time job at a bakery, she found George standing by the door of her car. He held out a white carnation, said, "Have a nice day," and turned as if to walk away. Then he turned back and held out a red rose. "Oh, and while you're at it, have a nice week." Then he vanished into the fog. George and the girl were going steady a month later.

The Secret to Nurturing Creativity in Others

Creative thinking starts with the right environment. If you want to give yourself, and the people in your life, a chance to exercise creativity, create an atmosphere that nourishes creative thinking. People do their best in an environment of safety and trust. This is the *only* kind of environment in which people will feel as though they're *allowed* to be creative. If people are afraid their ideas will be laughed at, stolen, or ignored, they won't share their brilliance.

Innovation comes from encouraging people to look for new options. Give yourself and others permission to share ideas. Ask for them. Listen to them carefully. Show people their ideas will be carefully considered. Build idea-sharing into meetings and casual conversations. Plan it as part of the routine. For these sessions, the rule is No Judgment. All ideas go up. We often find it hard not to comment—it brings up thoughts and everyone wants to blurt them out, but the only thing you can blurt out is another idea. One idea leads to another, and soon we have a "cluster." We draw bubbles around them and then make lines from one to another in a sort of burst.

Monty Roberts knows how to create an environment of trust and safety, to put those he works with at ease, to make them want to do their best. It's the secret to his success.

Monty works with horses. Where traditional methods of breaking a horse to saddle take four to six weeks, Monty can have a "wild" horse saddled and ready to ride in less than twenty-five minutes.

How does he do it?

He wins their trust. He speaks and moves in a way that inspires their confidence, that lets them know he cares about and understands their feelings. Instead of whipping the horse into submission and breaking its spirit, Monty gains the animal's trust by making it feel safe. Monty can read a horse so well that he knows when an animal will run away and when it can be approached and handled. He knows their "language," and knows how to "tell" them he's a friend. He can diagnose a problem horse's troubles and help it overcome the emotional stumbling block that's keeping it from a successful career. And he can inspire great horses to give their best efforts.

Rather than acting as a controller, Monty thinks of horses as athletes and works with them the way a coach would. He's trained some of the world's fastest horses. He believes his horses are successful because they *want* to race.

Solve Problems Creatively

Creativity is a powerful problem-solving tool. Because being creative is fun, solving problems creatively becomes a game, a satisfying form of entertainment, instead of a chore.

How do you harness your creativity and put it to work solving problems? It's a three-step process: (1) understand the problem, (2) generate ideas, and (3) plan for action. Let's take a closer look at each step:

Step 1: Understand the goal or problem. Define the situation. Determine the desirable outcome. Define parameters. What will it look like when you reach your goal or overcome the problem? Write everything down. Ask lots of questions—question everything, even the obvious. Dismantle the problem with the same rigorous curiosity and see what makes it go. Let's say you want to go to film school but you still have to contribute at least $2,000 a month toward your family's expenses. Write down the degree you'll have earned when you finish, the number of months it will take you, and the amount of money you'll need to bring in each month times the number of months.

Step 2: Generate ideas. The game at this stage in the process is to come up with as many ideas as possible. Don't evaluate at all during this phase, just scoop up as many ideas as you can—even the crazy ones. What you're practicing here is called *divergent thinking*: you're allowing your thoughts to go in many directions like a supernova. One idea leads to another. At this stage, they're all good. Write them all down. Banish judgment from this process. As I said earlier, creative thinkers generate ideas. If you get stuck, try consultant Steve Curtis's idea: say "I wish . . . " before coming up with your next idea, and let fly with whatever comes up.

Once you've gathered your ideas, cover and let simmer for a few hours or, if possible, a day. Abandonment, the act of disengaging temporarily, is an important part of the creative process. Author, producer, and literary manager Ken Atchity advises writers to take no fewer than *nine* planned "vacations" from revising their novels—each vacation with its own agenda. Even if you don't structure your time off to this degree, make sure you do plan for some moments away from the project. Go for a walk, play a video game, do something relaxing and repetitive. Sleep on it for a night or two if you can—good things come to the brainstorming process when you take it through a few dream cycles. At the very least, give yourself a moment of quiet reflection before you go to the next step. Ahas often come out of this incubation period.

After you've left your ideas alone for a while, turn up the heat. Go from simmer to full boil. Stir often. Sift through your ideas and examine them. Add insights as they occur. Note the ones that attract you the most. Start rummaging through and picking the ones that seem the most likely. Pull together the ones that seem related. What you're doing now is called *convergent thinking;* your ideas are contracting inward like a collapsing star. Soon your mix of ideas will be reduced to a small number of workable ones, then down to one.

I call this entire process "Slinky thinking" because the ideas expand and contract like a Slinky toy.

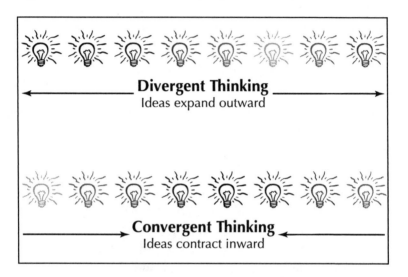

Step 3: Plan for action. After you've cooked your ideas down to one or two good ones, it's time to prepare for action. If it's a big plan, start with an overview so you won't lose your way.

Try storyboarding like moviemakers do. The legendary Walt Disney used the storyboarding process to make a map of the major moments in his movies. Adapt storyboarding to map the major moments in your plan.

Find a large piece of poster board or a big blank section of wall or floor. Write down the major milestones or categories in your plan. Then under each of these headers, draw a picture or write a description of each step in the process of achieving it.

Next, evaluate each portion of the plan. Ask yourself, "Is it working?" Get feedback. Fine-tune. Make necessary changes. Any time you come up against a barrier, return to the brainstorming phase and use it to improve the process.

Storyboarding Your Action Plan

The only difference between using your creativity to paint a landscape or write a poem and using it to come up with new ideas and solve problems is that one is a free-form expression and the other is applied. But it's the same skill and the same process.

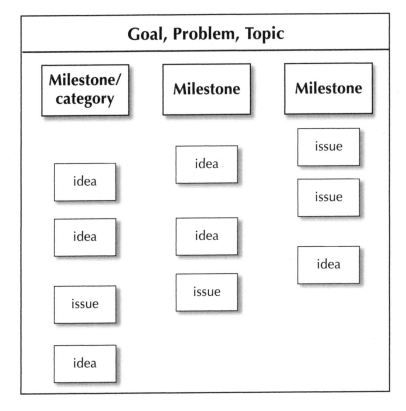

When you're applying creativity to a situation, don't get bogged down in the process, and don't let the "high" of creative thinking lure you off track. Stay focused on who you are, what you want, and what it will take to get there.

Our conference room is covered in whiteboards. We use colored markers and during planning, we often divide up into groups with each group taking a different board. Sometimes they have different problems and planning to work on, other times everyone has the same topic. Then, after a certain amount of time, each group presents. We once did this around the topic of "What are the top three qualities of a creative environment?" All four separate groups came up with the same top three attributes—independently of one another. By the time the last group presented, we were all in awe.

Their three qualities? Trust, respect, and fun.

Creative Thinking

- All human beings are creative: you're a human being; you're creative.
- Your creativity is a powerful tool for gaining understanding, solving problems, and looking at situations in a new way.
- Creativity is good for self-expression.
- Your creativity's of little use unless you're a doer: put your creativity into action.

CHAPTER 19

Maximize Your Memory

Your brain is capable of dazzling feats of memory if you
know a few simple memorization techniques and train it
to function at its best.

What You'll Discover in This Chapter:

- The keys to making your memory work for you
- What makes information memorable
- The master tools of maximizing memory

> *The true art of memory is the art of attention.*
> *—Samuel Johnson*

Public speaking didn't come naturally to me. The first time a friend asked me to address a group of about a hundred people, I was so eager to get it right I memorized the entire hour-long speech word-for-word. I found that when it came time to deliver the speech, the fact that all the words were in my head freed me up to focus on the meaning behind them and the connection I made to the audience. It gave me enormous confidence and the presentation just flowed. People said later my presentation was one of the highlights of the event. I don't recommend memorizing every word as a public speaking technique, and I certainly don't do this now that I have more experience. But at the time, it gave me the confidence boost I needed.

How did I hold that much text in my head? For one thing, I was driven by the sheer will to make a great presentation in spite of my nervousness. For another, I had a few powerful memorization techniques ready at hand. With the combination of strong will and training, you too can maximize your memory.

When I do seminars on memory, people surprise themselves with their own ability to remember things: "Wow! I memorized the periodic table! Wow! I just learned all the U.S. capitols!" You can get in on the fun, too, by tapping into your inner genius.

Every one of us has a hidden genius inside. All you have to do is unlock your potential.

You don't believe me? I'll explain.

We all share the same neurology. All human brains have approximately 100 billion nerve cells, each with axons and dendrites, the fibers that can connect one nerve cell to another. When you learn, you cause axons and dendrites to connect, forming a highway for information. The more you learn, the more connections you make. And the more you reinforce that learning, the stronger the connections become.

You, by the simple act of learning, have the ability to build yourself a super-brain.

How does it feel to have that kind of power?

> In *The New Brain: How the Modern Age is Rewiring Your Mind*, Dr. Richard Restak says, "People with extraordinary abilities . . . have learned to use their brains differently from the average person." What's the difference? Chess players, musical maestros, and others with extraordinary ability have taught themselves how to send information directly to their long-term memories.

Why Maximize Memory?

Why do you need a Quantum Memory to achieve Quantum Success? Because memory is one of the fuels that propels you toward the life you want.

The more you learn, the more you understand.

The more you understand, the better your decisions are.

The better your decisions, the more successful you are.

The more successful you are, the more joy and fulfillment you find.

A little addendum to this quatrain is the fact that joy and fulfillment lead you to desire to learn more, which starts the cycle all over again. It's an endless spiral upward.

> The two most important things to do when you're memorizing something:
>
> **Pay attention:** Be clear and aware of what you want to remember. Repeat a person's name in your head if you want to remember it. Write out lists you need to memorize.

Make associations: Make clear, conscious connections. Be specific, concrete, and visual. Visual associations are usually more powerful than rhymes, although some rhymes do stick, like "Thirty days has September." But images are faster and clearer.

You Learn Best When You Know Why You're Learning

The more important a piece of information is to you, the better you learn. If you want to acquire a certain chunk of knowledge, make sure you tell yourself why you're acquiring it.

Neuropsychologist Larry Squire of the University of California, San Diego, studies the brain processes involved in memory. He found that the hippocampus plays a large role in cataloging and storing memories. It temporarily records events, then decides which memories will go to long-term storage and how they'll be stored.

Researcher Robert Sylwester of the University of Oregon says the hippocampus is like a librarian cataloging, filing, and storing away information. The hippocampus needs a strong enough reason to move information to long-term storage. If the reason isn't compelling enough to convince the hippocampus, out it goes. The more convinced the hippocampus is of an item's importance, the stronger and faster the retrieval system it will build for that item. Let's say you're at a party and you meet about a dozen new people. How many of their names and faces will you remember? But then your friend introduces you to the hiring manager at a company you've always wanted to work with. You'll remember *this* person's name and face long after the others are forgotten.

You learn the best when you know what's in it for you. The more you know about why you're adapting to a new circumstance or acquiring new knowledge, the more successfully you'll learn it.

When you want to acquire information, find your WIIFM: What's In It For Me. Pick the strongest WIIFM you can find.

Invent one if you have to. Someone gives you directions to a safe containing $2 million in gold bullion—yours if you remember how to get to it. If you have a WIIFM that strong, you'll hang onto the information!

Your Brain's Librarian

The hippocampus, a seahorse-shape structure inside your brain, sorts, categorizes, and stores your memories. It decides what's important enough to keep and what's not. You can signal your hippocampus that information is significant by marking the information you acquire with a big sign that says IMPORTANT! KEEP!

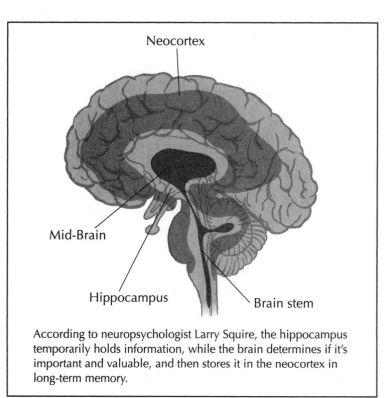

Neocortex

Mid-Brain

Hippocampus

Brain stem

According to neuropsychologist Larry Squire, the hippocampus temporarily holds information, while the brain determines if it's important and valuable, and then stores it in the neocortex in long-term memory.

At SuperCamp we teach the ABCs of learning: A is for Attitude, B for Belief, and C for concentration. Attitude is your orientation toward learning, your ability to take responsibility and own your adaptation process. Belief refers to belief in yourself—in your ability to acquire and apply new knowledge. Concentration means putting yourself in a calm, focused alpha state, the best frame of mind from which to learn.

Survival might be the most motivating WIIFM, but there's another WIIFM that brings deeper, longer-term satisfaction: *intrinsic motivation.*

What's intrinsic motivation? It's like a quantum WIIFM. It's a WIIFM so deep that it's part of you, something that speaks to the core of who you are. When you tap into your intrinsic motivation, you learn with energy, joy, and a sensation that your learning was meant to be. You experience the sensation of being at the heart of the universe.

I experience intrinsic motivation whenever I'm learning something about the way people learn. It's my life's work. I don't have to struggle with my willpower to acquire new knowledge about learning because I feel most at home when I'm absorbed in this subject. My friend who loves wine has an astonishing head for wine lore; she can absorb a mind-boggling number of facts about wine varieties and vintages simply because it's her passion. Another friend, a triathlete, can rattle off race statistics and times down to fractions of a minute for events that happened several weeks ago. It's the subject that dominates her thinking most of the time. Her brain is always ready to receive race-related information.

The stronger your incentive, the higher your commitment level. The best possible scenario for learning is when your WIIFM is related to both your survival and your fulfillment. That's a message your hippocampus can't ignore!

Go for the Aha

Our brains become more "dense," more connected, as we continue to have those Aha moments of learning.

The Master-Memory Tools of Accelerated Acquisition

My son Grant thinks memorizing is fun. He memorizes things just for entertainment—and of course it's great practice. Out of the blue, he'll challenge me to name all the U.S. presidents—in order. License plates, the Seven Dwarfs, whatever. It's fun to him. But he swears it helped him get a high score on his SAT and get his MBA. Now president of HC Restaurant Group, Grant uses these techniques daily to remember the names of the many people he meets, food items, sports trivia, and numbers (he once memorized over a thousand menu item codes on a long flight).

How does he do it? He uses a handful of simple techniques that he has mastered.

One of Grant's daughters came home from school upset because, in her mind, she was the only one in her class who didn't know the months of the year by heart. *Why* couldn't she memorize them? Grant told her a silly story. He cheered her up, made her laugh, and asked her to repeat parts of the story. "That's *easy*, Daddy." He'd given her a little confidence boost along the way. Immediately on hearing it, she said she knew the whole thing by heart. It started with a girl named Jan. It was very cold and Jan was wearing a fake fur coat called a "Furberry" (try finishing it!).

Her dad smiled. "I think you also know the months of the year."

He then showed her how the information was embedded in the story, one month "pinned" to each element in the story. It was all there in her memory already.

Her eyes lit up and she ran out the door yelling, "Mom, I know the months!"

Mental Stickies: Eight Ways to Hold On to Memory

I call the following eight elements Mental Stickies because they make information stick. The categories are Sensory, Intense, Outstanding, Emotional, Survival, Repetition, Personal Importance, and First and Last. Let's examine each of these:

1. Sensory: You create the strongest memories by combining your experience of sight, sound, smell, taste, and touch. Focus on motion, colors, tones. Take time to see things clearly in your mind. See items moving together. Listen attentively. Recall through touch—remember having to "dial" a phone number to bring it to memory? Use smell to trigger memory, especially the emotional tone of memory. Layer your associations with as many of your five senses as possible.

2. Intense: To make your acquisition memorable, make it intense. Exaggerate it, make it absurd, wildly colorful, even sexual. Remember a speech by imagining the speaker talking like Donald Duck. Change scale: think of an enormous fly or a tiny elephant. Exaggerate movements. Just make sure you keep the images positive. Your brain wants you to forget negative experiences.

3. Outstanding: To make a piece of information stick, make it stick *out*. Imagine that it stands out in extreme contrast from other things around it. If you want to remember one person out of a group, imagine that she's wearing orange while everybody else is wearing blue.

4. Emotional: Add an emotional layer to the information you're acquiring. Images charged with love, happiness, and laughter are easy to remember. Connect the information you're acquiring to a

positive feeling. Make a joke or a visual pun connected with the item you want to remember. For instance, if you want to remember that the hippocampus is the librarian of your brain, visualize a doughty hippo in bifocals and a beehive wig, busily arranging books on a library shelf.

5. Survival: Your strongest possible motivation is survival. Talk about being motivated to remember! Find a way to link the knowledge to your need for food, shelter, safety, health, or companionship. If you need to remember a piece of information for your job, tie it to the fact that you need your paycheck to pay your bills.

6. Personal Importance: Link the information you're acquiring to something personal. Associate it with a cherished friend, family member, favorite event, or object that's special to you. Let's say you have to remember a particular door on a street with no visible address numbers. The door is little distinguished from those around it, except that it's blue. You recall that your godmother Maria, whom you adored, lived in a little house with a blue door. You remember which door is the correct one because you associate it with your godmother.

7. Repetition: Mere repetition can help with the short term, but if you really want information to stick, try repeating it in different ways, in different orders, and with more intense focus. Sing it as a song. Make it rhyme and turn it into a poem. Or chant it as a slogan. A friend's third-grader will always remember the special word for the number 144 because his teacher taught the students to yell "Gross!" every time someone spoke the number aloud.

8. First and Last: You remember best the first and last things you learn in a sequence. When you meet a new group of people, you're most likely to remember the name of the person you met first and the person you met last. Tap into the power of this natural tendency by creating more firsts and lasts. Take short, frequent

breaks—at least every thirty minutes—so that each half hour has a built-in first and last.

You remember best when you combine two or more of these categories. For instance, let's say you need to remember the layout of a three-story office building. Now instead of remembering the building as glass, steel, and concrete, make the memory intense: Turn it into a layer cake. Each floor is a different flavor: the ground floor is chocolate, the second floor, strawberry, the third, vanilla. As you remember which departments are on each floor of your building-cake, bring in the sensory dimension of taste—imagine the flavor of each layer. The more categories a piece of information can fit into, the more likely you are to hold onto it.

Let's look at a few more techniques for achieving Quantum Memory:

Association: Association is used in all memory techniques. Reinforce a piece of information you want to acquire by associating it with a familiar object. For instance, when we teach Mental Stickies in our seminars, we encourage people to associate them with characters from *The Wizard of Oz*. Dorothy is Sensory since we experience the movie through her, Tin Man is Emotional because he yearns for a heart, First and Last is Auntie Em and Uncle Henry because they appear at the beginning and end of the movie, and so forth. Wine expert Karen MacNeil helps her students remember types of wine by associating their characteristics with those of their favorite movie stars: Chardonnay is full-bodied and sensuous like Marilyn Monroe, Shiraz is ruggedly elegant like Jack Palance, and Pinot Noir is sultry like Catherine Zeta-Jones.

Linking: When you're acquiring a string of information, like a sequence of steps, you'll learn them best by linking one piece of information to the next. A friend's grade-school sons came home singing a little nonsense song. My friend surprised herself by accidentally memorizing the song after one hearing. She later realized it was because the song's lines were linked: "Ooh, ai, I wanna piece of pie. Pie too sweet, I wanna piece of meat. Meat too tough, I wanna ride a bus. Bus too full, I wanna ride a bull ..." This song uses both rhyming and picturing the items in your mind.

Location: Another way to fix information in your mind is to associate them with locations. For instance, we use body location to remember the 8 Key Catalysts, starting with placing both hands on top of our heads for Values and Actions. We associate Failure Leads to Success with our noses because of the "sweet smell of success." We associate Speak with Good Purpose with our mouths, This Is It with our chins (chins in the air), Commitment with our arms (showing our muscles), Ownership with hands on our stomachs (taking ownership of what we put in our bodies), Flexibility with our (bended) knees, and Balance with our feet. Note that we started at the top and worked down to keep the items in a particular order. You remember best when items are in order.

Home Is a Powerful Place for Memory

I use locations in my home to help me remember things. Think about your own home. You know it well! Think about how you would naturally walk through your home. I always walk through mine in the same direction so I always know what's next. Being specific is a key to remembering. I start with my front door, then my front hallway. Next, the living room, dining room, kitchen, staircase, master bedroom, bath, next bedroom, back downstairs, and out the door to the back yard. In each space I can associate things in the room with topics. I use this to prepare for meetings and speeches. I chunk the content, then associate a chunk with each space. If I'm in my dining room, I'll attach one item to my table, another to the vase on the table, and another to the light switch on the wall.

Have fun practicing these techniques, but don't stop here! The world is full of memory-boosting strategies and as you develop your remarkable Quantum Memory, you'll probably add a few of your own memorizing systems to the world.

After all, you *are* a genius.

Maximize Your Memory

- There's some form of genius in all of us.
- The more you learn, the more "connections" your brain makes.
- You can turbocharge your learning with a super-strong WIIFM.
- You can power-load information into your long-term memory by experiencing it with as many senses as possible, on as many experiential levels as possible.

PART V

Live Your Quantum Success:
Meaning Is the Reason
for the Ride

CHAPTER 20

Quantum Joy: Live What Lights You Up

Talent for talent's sake is a bauble and a show.
Talent working with joy in the cause of universal truth
lifts the possessor to new power as a benefactor.
—Ralph Waldo Emerson

Quantum Success is living with joy. It's about being fulfilled, in love with yourself and your place in the world, about being happy, making a difference, and doing what you love. This is how the ride feels.

What does your Quantum Success look like?

Throughout the book, I've been showing you mine. What I want to leave you with most is the joy that I experience, and the way my life flows. I have no desire to retire because I love doing what I'm doing. People retire so they can enjoy life; I *am* enjoying life! I'm living who I am.

Quantum Success is less about *what* you do and all about how you do it. It's about doing the greatest and smallest of things with meaning and mission. Remember the bus driver who told all his passengers to shout "I am somebody!" Remember Apple's Steve Jobs entering the most creative phase of his life after his fall from grace in the corporate world. Remember Maria Montessori, Jane Goodall, J.K. Rowling, and my friend the wine expert. What unites their stories is the rapture they experienced in creating something greater than themselves *from* themselves.

I recently returned from a trip to the Dominican Republic overwhelmed with appreciation for what we are able to do. We had just held a SuperCamp for poor and abused kids, some of whom lived and worked in a garbage dump, many of whom had never been out of their barrios before. The grant that funded the program there provided them with clothes and toothbrushes. By the end of the program, these previously isolated kids were bright, shining, laughing, dancing, and learning. The vice president of the country visited during the program and told me, "You're changing education."

Whether it's poor kids in the Dominican Republic or affluent kids at Stanford, I see the change that occurs in them when they discover their ability to follow their dreams. This is what fulfills me the most.

What fulfills you?

This is your time to shine. In working through your dreams, passions, and desires, you've come face to face with the wondrous creation you are and the unique gifts you have to offer the world. You're a radiant example of integrity, responsibility, commitment, and flexibility. You exist in the present moment. You speak with good purpose. And you're able to maneuver and adapt to change without losing your balance—even in the midst of this supercharged electronic avalanche we call the twenty-first century.

Quantum Success is about who you are as a person. It's a shift in the way you exist in the world that changes everything else. It starts with awareness. This book demonstrates that when you bring self-awareness together with vision, values, passion, and a thirst for knowledge, you create a quantum shift—a shift in who you are as a person.

The ideas I've discussed in this book dovetail with one other. Balance, for instance, goes hand in hand with integrity—which gets its frame of reference from your values. A sense of imbalance is one of the first signs that your behaviors aren't in line with your vision. In the same way, commitment can guide you back to ownership. Flexibility and commitment may seem to contradict one another, but when they're in service to a vision, they become complementary, showing you where to bend and where to hold firm. The purpose of all of these ideas is to guide you back to your own vision. Whenever your vision calls for action, you can mobilize your brainstorming, planning, and acquisition skills. The whole equation together creates a seamless package.

Let's say, for instance, you start a new venture and fail. Since you own your own actions, you don't waste time blaming anyone for your failure. You can tap into your knowledge that failure leads to success. You can diagnose your failure and create a new action plan using Mind Mapping or any of the other adaptation techniques you've learned. Then you can dip into your toolbox of knowledge acquisition techniques and find the information that will get you over the roadblock that led to your failure. You respond to your failures with action because you're aware that this is it—this moment is the only one that matters.

Put Your Life into Harmony

Wherever you are in your own ride, think of yourself, always, as a work in progress. One of our Quantum Learning facilitators, John Letellier, tells participants, "If you think you're green, you're growing; if you think you're ripe, you're rotten." Since we're all perpetually green, we could all use more practice. And the more you practice the lessons you've learned in this book, the more they'll pay you back.

How do you practice them? By thinking, talking, exploring, and reflecting. It starts with being aware and "remembering to remember." I notice that when I learn something new or focus on something, at first it seems like all I do is the opposite. It's just because I'm now aware of what I had been doing unconsciously. For instance, I like for people to get to the point and I've been known to finish people's sentences or cut them off. I'm working on it. Now when I do it, it's as if I'm looking down on myself from above. It's my voice in my head saying, "Look, you just did it again!" Over time, I'm doing it less.

Think about what you've learned. Reflect on moments in your life and see how these principles might have applied. Talk about them with your family, friends, and coworkers. You could discuss one concept or technique from this book each week. You might ask each person to give a short presentation on something they've learned from it, or ask people to come up with anecdotes that illustrate that element in action. In my company, a different staff member presents a key talk every other week at our meetings. I know of a school where a different key is embedded into the curriculum each month and students receive key awards. The goal: increased awareness, followed by change and competence.

Make periodic self-assessments. Revisit your vision—is your plan still in line? How well are you living the 8 Key Catalysts? When was the last time you brushed up on your accelerated acquisition techniques?

At my company, I offer an assessment that allows staffers to check their use of the 8 Key Catalysts. For each statement, they answer Always, Mostly, Sometimes, or Almost Never:

Live What You Value
I have stated beliefs and values.
I know and understand them.
My behavior reflects them.

Failure Leads to Success
I'm not afraid to make mistakes.
When I make them, I take the time to learn from them.
I believe failures are opportunities for growth.

Speak with Good Purpose

I speak with good intent—no swearing, put-downs, or gossip.

I'm honest and direct.

I walk my talk.

This Is It!

I'm focused on my goals and objectives.

I make every moment count.

I acknowledge and accept where I am in good and bad times.

Commit Yourself

I have a clear vision and I stay true to it.

I do whatever it takes to get the job done.

I can be counted on to keep my word.

Take Ownership

I'm accountable for my actions.

I take responsibility.

I see what needs to be done and do it.

Stay Flexible

I change strategies when I need to do so to achieve my goals.

When something isn't working, I try another way.

I ask for help when I need it.

Keep Your Balance

I give to the things that are important to me the amount of time that creates the greatest sense of fulfillment.

Use this checklist whenever you feel the need—to give yourself a tune-up and a refresher course, and to help you integrate the 8 Key Catalysts more deeply into your life. A staff member once wrote me about what happened to her after she left SuperCamp. She said she had planned to "live the 8 Keys" when she was at camp, but to go back to her old way of life when she returned home. But when she got back home she found she couldn't go back to the way she had been living. The 8 Keys had become part of her—which is exactly what they're meant to do.

The more you read, think about, practice, and share the concepts in the book, the more you'll see them entwining to create a solid fabric within your life. You can't work with them and not incorporate them. After a while, you'll find them popping up to assist you in all kinds of situations, large and small.

I hope you to come away from the experience of reading this book with a sense of joy for who you are and for what you're here to do. I hope you find the rapture and fulfillment of living what lights you up and shifting your energy into dynamic focus.

The ride is yours for the taking. Enjoy!

I was born a long way from where I'm supposed to be,
so I'm on my way home.
—Bob Dylan

Permissions

Other Books
by Bobbi DePorter

The 8 Keys of Excellence: Principles to Live By. Learning Forum
Publications, 2000.

Quantum Writing: How to Write Like a Pro. Learning Forum
Publications, 2000.

Quantum Reading: The Power to Read Your Best. Learning Forum
Publications, 2000.

Quantum Pathways: Discovering Your Personal Learning Style.
Learning Forum Publications, 2000.

Quantum Notes: Whole-Brain Approaches to Note-Taking. Learning
Forum Publications, 2000.

*Quantum Thinking: Creative Thinking, Planning, and Problem-
Solving.* Learning Forum Publications, 2000.

Quantum Memory: Working Magic with Your Memory. Learning
Forum Publications, 2000.

with Mike Hernacki:

Quantum Business: Achieving Success Through Quantum Learning.
Dell Trade Paperback, 1997.

Quantum Learning: Unleashing the Genius in You. Dell Trade
Paperback, 1992.

with Mark Reardon and Sara Singer-Nouri:

Quantum Teaching: Orchestrating Student Success. Allyn & Bacon,
1999.

How to Contact the Quantum Learning Network

By Phone: (760) 722-0072

By Mail: Quantum Learning Network
      1938 Avenida del Oro
      Oceanside, CA 92056

Online: www.QLN.com

International associate offices in Taiwan, China, Hong Kong, South Korea, Malaysia, Singapore, Indonesia, Mexico, Dominican Republic, and Switzerland.

For a free ebook: *8 Keys—More Stories*, go to www.QLN.com/QuantumSuccess

QLN quantum learning network™
supercamp QLN education QLN business
QLN family   QLN products   QLN worldwide